Communicative Ideas

An approach with classroom activities

David Norman
Ulf Levihn
Jan Anders Hedenquist

Language Teaching Publications
35 Church Road Hove BN3 2BE

Acknowledgement
Some of the ideas in this book first appeared in *Språka*, published by
Liberförlag in Sweden in Swedish. The ideas have been extensively
developed and revised for the present work.
We are grateful to Punch for permission to reproduce several cartoons.

David Norman, Ulf Levihn, Jan Anders Hedenquist
ISBN 0 906717 38 8

Typeset by London Overload, 14-17 Wells Mews, London W1.
In 10pt Times Roman Nr. 1.

Printed in England by Commercial Colour Press, London E7.

Introduction

Communicative Ideas is written in English, but addresses itself as much to teachers of French, Spanish, Italian, German — in fact, of all foreign languages.

The book provides the busy teacher with a wide range of practical and imaginative ways of adding variety to any basic method. It may serve as a complementary source of inspiration to any basic textbook.

The activities cover all levels, from beginners to advanced. We believe that most of these activities can be used equally well in any kind of teaching environment - schools, (state or private), language teaching institutes, adult education, company or business courses and so on.

The methodology of **Communicative Ideas** stresses, more than other books of a similar kind, student participation, creativity, students producing their own materials, fun and games and subconscious language acquisition.

Communicative Ideas has two sections:

> — Techniques
> — Activities

The *Techniques* section gives a general, more theoretical, introduction to the *Activities* section. It contains general information about organising language studies in the groups or classes. It makes specific reference to some of the *Activities* that follow. This section has been made more activating for the individual reader by the inclusion of questions and tasks. These may also be used for group discussions on language teaching in general.

It is widely believed that motivation is the key to successful learning. Although motivation comes largely from within the individual, certain external factors (success/failure, encouragement, anxiety, rewards) can have a positive or negative influence. In order to create the best possible environment for language skills to develop, the activities in this book have been chosen with the following aims in mind:

> — to promote student activity and co-operation
> — to reduce stress and individual anxiety
> — to focus on the students' own interests and creative abilities.

These aims, and suggestions for achieving them, are discussed in the *Techniques* section.

The *Activities* section contains a large number of language activities. They are loosely divided into groups, but overlapping often occurs as an activity may be, for example, both a listening and a discussion activity. This emphasises the flexibility of many of the activities and the universality of the skills involved. The emphasis is on oral skills, but many different writing practices are also suggested. Most of the activities are game-orientated, or contain an element of fun. Almost all are designed to include pair or group work.

Within each group the shorter and easier activities tend to occur first and the longer, more difficult activities later, but this is only a guide.

Each activity is described in the following way:

Language skills

These are described in general terms according to the type of activity. If particular language items are given, the examples are usually given in English.

Procedure

A step-by-step explanation of how to carry out the activity. The basic procedure is adaptable to all languages. This universality of approach is one of the features of the book.

Comments

This explains the rationale behind the activity. It discusses both content and method and offers further practical tips, often in the form of *Variations*.

Two terms are used in the book which may need further explanation:
L1 = the language normally used by the students, their
native language
L2 = the language being studied by the class, the target
language.
The activities in the book cover an extensive range. Some are grammatical; some are based on texts; some are totally student-created; some are very simple; some very general, such as "The Block of Flats" (page 119). All have been tested in a variety of teaching situations. They have been collected from a wide range of language teaching sources. Some are original, others not. We hope you will find plenty to stimulate, provoke, amuse and, above all, to generate ideas for practising the skills of communication.

Finally, we would like to express our gratitude to Paul Thomas for his con-siderable help in the initial stage of work on this material, and for contributing the ideas for some of the activities - likewise to Michael Lewis for his contributions in revising and, in some cases, adding to the material in the *Activities* section.

Ulf Levihn   Jan Anders Hedenquist   David Norman

Techniques

Phases in language teaching

The language teaching process can be divided into a number of 'phases'. First the new language is *introduced* in some way, then students *practise* it and finally there is some form of *follow-up*:

Input → Practice → Follow-up

- Have you met this idea before of dividing up the teaching process into phases? ☐ **Yes** ☐ **No**
- Have you used other terms for these phases?

  If so, what? _____

  _____

- What is the main aim of

  1. the input phase? _____

  _____

  2. the practice phase? _____

  _____

  3. the follow-up phase? _____

  _____

- Does this 3-phase division cover the process adequately? ☐ **Yes** ☐ **No**

  If **No,** what other phases would you include? ___

  _____

- Where in the process would you include, for example, the following phases?
  Review   **Analysis of Needs**   **Extension**

  _____

6

Techniques

1. The Input Phase

It is confusing to introduce too much language at once. It is often better to take one item at a time — such as new vocabulary, a new grammatical structure or a pronunciation point — and then combine and contextualize.

> ● Do you agree with the above viewpoint?
>
> ☐ **Yes**   ☐ **No**

The alternative is to begin with the whole and then examine the parts.

> ● What are the arguments for or against either of these approaches?
>
> _____
>
> _____
>
> ● Which approach do you usually use for the input phase?
>
> _____
>
> _____

The input phase can be carried out — in the whole class
　　　　　　　　　　　　　　　　　　— in pairs or small groups
　　　　　　　　　　　　　　　　　　— individually

1a. Input — in the whole class

This may be the quickest way of presenting new language material, but how efficient is it? It may mean many students listen badly, or to only part of the presentation.

The teacher may not be aware of how much students already know. Do students have the opportunity to ask about something they have not understood if this phase takes place in the whole class? Do students *dare* to ask in front of everyone else? The larger the audience, the greater the nervousness, and fear of making a fool of oneself. To ask something which other students may think is "stupid" demands considerable courage.

> ● What is your reaction to the above?
>
> ☐ generally agree ☐ not sure ☐ strongly disagree
>
> ● What alternatives are there?_____
>
> _____

When planning the input phase the following points should be considered:

1. What is to be introduced?

- new vocabulary
- new grammar
- new intonation patterns

- _____
- _____
- _____

(own examples)

2. Is the input to be managed by . . .

- the teacher
- a group of students
- one student
- a tape recorder

- inferring directly from the material
- _____
- _____
- _____

(own examples)

3. How is the new language material to be explained?

- by examples or patterns
- by illustrations
- by translating into L1
- by explaining (in L1 or L2)

- by gestures or mime
- _____
- _____
- _____

(own examples)

> - Which are you **most** familiar with?
> - Which have you **not** tried?

Situations in which activities in the whole class may be appropriate:

- when introducing a new type of activity or method
- when giving information
- when demonstrating pronunciation and intonation
- when planning and making decisions prior to further work on a task.

1b. Input — in pairs or small groups

The first introduction to any new language material can be carried out in pairs or small groups. Students can get help from each other, from word lists, tapes or from the explanations and comments in the material itself. If they have problems, they can ask the teacher. After going through the material, the pairs or groups may compare with each other.

What advantages or disadvantages does this method offer compared to the teacher presenting to the whole class?

- The students are likely to be more active.
- There is more opportunity for the students to help each other instead of sitting alone, struggling to understand.
- It is generally easier to show that you do not know, or do not understand something, in a smaller group than in a large one.
- Group presentation may take longer but the extra time and effort usually means better understanding and assimilation of the material.

> - Can you think of any further advantages?
> - Can you find any disadvantages?

Conducting the Input phase in pairs or small groups is particularly appropriate:

- for active study of new material such as text or vocabulary.

- in meeting the different needs of students. Each pair or group can choose to concentrate on their difficulties and translate, check in a dictionary or ask for the particular help they need.

- in preparing a task after which a summary or list can be made in the whole class.

- for active study of new grammar, using deductive techniques or the 'discovery method' in understanding structural patterns and formulating rules. (See Activity 11, Page 35).

1c. Input — working individually

Individual work on the input phase may be done as homework or classwork. In the latter case, the following procedure may be adopted:

1. Each student works quietly on the given material, making notes (in L1 or L2) on any difficulties, commenting, summarising, etc.

2. Afterwards any problems can be taken up in pairs, small groups or the whole class.

If material has been prepared in this way by the students working on their own, the short follow-up should be meaningful and relevant to the students' needs.

2. The Practice Phase

The main purpose of the practice phase in language teaching is give the students the opportunity to practise and use the new language input in a variety of forms.

Success in language learning is in direct proportion to the length of time spent in practising the language and on the quality of that practice.

● Do you agree with the above statement?

☐ Yes, completely ☐ Not at all ☐ Partially

● How much of your lesson time do you estimate is devoted to active practice of L2 on the part of the students?

☐ Up to 30% ☐ 30-60%
☐ 60-80% ☐ More than 80%

● What is the ratio of guided/controlled practice to free practice? Make an estimate of an average lesson (e.g. 60-40%) _____

● Which language skills is most of the practice time devoted to? Rank in order of average time spent per lesson. (from 1 to 4)

_____ Reading _____ Speaking
_____ Listening _____ Writing

In the past, language teaching often followed the pattern:

Teacher reads or explains ➜ Pupils listen, repeat, read or translate.

Activities usually took place in the whole class context, or with the students working individually.

● What disadvantages may there be in this procedure?

Language practice should aim to achieve:

● Maximum student activity
● Maximum co-operation and communication between students
● Freedom from anxiety and tension on the part of the students — a relaxed atmosphere

---

● Do you agree with these basic aims of the practice phase?
● What implications do they have as regards teaching techniques and lesson planning?

Activity

Learning pre-supposes activity on the part of the learner. Nobody can learn to swim without getting into the water!

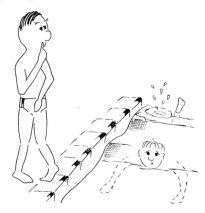

Nobody learns to drive by sitting beside the driver; you have to get into the driving seat yourself. Activity in language learning involves the use of the skills of listening, speaking, reading and writing. It is seldom, however, that these skills are practised in isolation. Instead, for communication to take place, some more general process such as interpreting is involved. Thus:

Listening ⟷ Interpreting ⟷ Speaking
(Conversation)

Reading ⟷ Interpreting ⟷ Writing
(Written correspondence)

In order to develop this communicative aspect of language, skills should be practised in different combinations rather than in isolation. For example:

    Listening (eg to a tape recording)
➜ *Writing* (eg taking notes)
➜ *Speaking* (eg reporting, comparing, discussing)
➜ *Writing* (eg summarising).

> ● How many different combinations can you think of? Draw diagrams as in the example below.

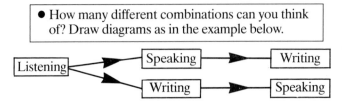

Many of the activities in this book are designed to exploit various ways of practising the different skills involved in language communication. Modern theories of learning stress the importance of engaging both hemispheres of the brain and of using as many of the senses as possible. It is generally believed that the left side of the brain handles logic — mathematics — language — analysis — writing, etc. and that the right side of the brain deals with imagination — colour — music — rhythm — daydreaming, etc.

Activities which stimulate *both* sides tend to achieve better results than activities which concentrate on one. Similarly, by engaging different senses in a practice activity (touch, smell, taste, as well as hearing and sight), learning tends to be reinforced. Language practice should therefore aim at activating the whole individual and not simply the intellect. Language learning involves both conscious effort, using grammatical rules and exercises for example, and also subconscious acquisition. Many activities in this book, particularly in the second half, promote language acquistion as opposed to conscious learning.

Co-operation

Most people learn a foreign language better with others than on their own. Learning a language requires more than the understanding of words and grammatical rules (linguistic competence). It requires the ability to put this knowledge into practice (communicative competence).

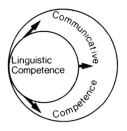

Language practice should therefore provide opportunities for students to co-operate, communicate and interact with one another in a variety of ways. The activities must feel meaningful and realistic to the students. Presenting such activities is one of the principal aims of this book. (see *Information Gaps, Page 100* for a good example)

- What do you understand by the term 'communicative competence'?
- In what practical ways can co-operation be promoted in the language lesson?
- Find examples in the activities described in this book.
- Can a foreign language be learned without interacting with others?

Techniques

Freedom from anxiety and tension

One of the basic principles of some modern teaching methods such as Sug-gestopedia and Community Language Learning, is the creation of a relaxed atmosphere to counteract feelings of anxiety and tension on the part of the learners. Various techniques are employed to promote this atmosphere.

> ● Can you list any techniques to use in creating a
>   relaxed atmosphere in the learning situation?

Research indicates that learning under stress is often ineffective and can even be of negative value. It also suggests that the smaller the group, the lower the level of stress.

Most people are timid and uncertain when asked to perform in front of an audience. It is much easier to function in a small group. In the context of the language lesson it is generally true to say that the smaller the group, the greater the activity level of each individual student. On the other hand, a larger group expresses a greater variety of opinions and covers a wider range of knowledge and experience. The choice of group size for language practice activities will depend largely on the size of the class and the aim and type of activity in question. A combination of pairwork - groupwork - whole class is often most effective.

> ● What kinds of tasks/activities are best suited for
>   pairwork?
> ● What activities are best for larger groups?

Confidence can often be built up best by *progressing* from individual work to pair work and finally to performing in larger groups.

Here are some examples of ways of reducing tensions:

- games/fun activities
- listening to music
- role-playing
- encouraging student initiative and creativity
- performing tasks that are interesting in themselves

At the same time this type of activity focuses attention away from the actual language learning and towards the activity itself. This is called *de-focusing*. The result is to encourage more subconscious learning, concentrating more on *what* to say than *how* to say it.

> ● Do you agree with the above list?
> ● Go back and check with your own list.
> ● Find examples from the Activities in this book.
>
> _____
>
> _____

Examples of different forms of practice

> - Below are illustrations of different forms of practice. Evaluate each one in turn.
> - Which ones are most likely to —
>
>   promote student activity?
>   promote co-operation between students?
>   reduce tension and anxiety?

Represents an active student, one performing a task (speaking, reporting, writing, etc)

Represents other students - ie those not actually performing, but often listening.

A
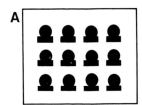

B
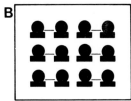

C
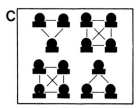

Individual practice -
students working on
their own

Pairwork -
practice in pairs

Group work -
practice in small groups

In each of these three forms work is done *simultaneously* in groups, pairs or individually. The noise level or hum of activity may be disturbing at first but one soon grows accustomed to it. It also reflects 'real life' in, for example, a restaurant or shop, in the street or at a party.

D
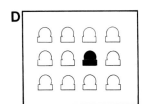

E
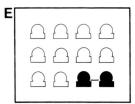

F
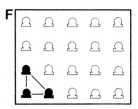

One student
'performing' in front of
the whole class

One pair 'performing'
in front of
the whole class

One group 'performing'
in front of the class

> - "Combinations D-F are more suited as forms of follow-up rather than practice".
>   Do you agree? Why/why not?
>
> - How can the students who are not 'performing' in D-F be made more active?
>
> - What is the teacher's role in the practice phase?

There are, of course, two more possibilities — individual practice, such as a student working at home, and the whole group active at the same time, for example, doing choral pronunciation.

2a. Individual practice

This form of practice means that each student works alone without talking to, or co-operating with, others. It is used sparingly when studying a language in a group/class, but can serve as a preliminary to further forms of practice or follow-up. It gives everyone an opportunity to practise the material in question undisturbed by others.

2b. Pair practice

This form of practice, with all pairs working simultaneously, provides the maximum of student activity and co-operation. It creates a feeling of security as students can support and help each other. The risk of 'making a fool of oneself' in front of other people is reduced.

Most language textbooks nowadays include pair work activities. It is natural that it should play a prominent role in language studies — language is in reality very often a conversation between two people.

Of course most teachers are familiar with pair work to practise dialogues and information gap activities. Teachers do not always recognise, however, that pair practice is equally, even especially, suited to most types of:

- text work
- grammar exercises
- vocabulary work

In short, as soon as teachers leave the traditional whole-class activity and develop a variety of pair practices, students are more active, and the practice is likely to be more effective.

2c. Practice in small groups

A school class can easily be divided into smaller units for the practice phase of a lesson. Even a small class or group can with advantage be divided into smaller units. The result should be increased activity, co-operation and a greater sense of security for each student.

Practice in small groups is particularly suited for activities directed towards

- discussion
- freer conversation
- role-play
- problem-solving
- drama

2d. Practice in whole class

Although in many situations this is still the most common type of practice, it is generally inadvisable to practise in the whole class context. The majority of the students are more or less inactive, little or no co-operation takes place and the student or students who are performing are put at risk.

This form of practice may be used for

- choral repetition — for pronunciation/intonation practice
- illustrating or demonstrating an exercise before practising in smaller groups
- training to speak in public (meetings, conferences, etc)

> - Summarise the advantages and disadvantages of the different forms of practice outlined above.

3. The follow-up Phase

A practice session is generally followed up in some way.

> - Do you normally include a follow-up in your lesson planning? ☐ Yes ☐ No
> - What form does it usually take?
> - Make a list of all the basic aims you can think of for this phase.
>
> _____
>
> _____
>
> _____
>
> - What are the consequences if this phase is omitted or if inadequate time is devoted to it?
>
> _____

The aims and form of the follow-up phase will depend to a large extent on the work done during the previous phases. The degree of difficulty involved, the scope for creativity and the amount of control of the preceding activities will influence the choice and form of follow-up work.

Some aims of follow-up work:

- a *check* on the input and practice phases

  (What have the students learned? What needs to be reviewed?)

- the *sharing* of information from tasks done individually or in groups

- the *integration* or *extension* of items/skills practised elsewhere

- a *review* of language input and skills practised to aid memorisation

> - What means can be used of presenting group work carried out in the practice phase?

Just as in the input and practice phases, the follow-up can be carried out:

- individually
- in the whole class
- in pairs or small groups
- in cross-reporting groups

3a. Follow-up in the whole class

One student, or a pair or group of students read, act or report on their task while the rest of the class listens. Another student, pair or group then continues, and so on.

3b. Follow-up in pairs or small groups

Most students feel less nervous if the practice phase can be followed up together with another student or in a small group rather than in front of the whole class. Access to support material, such as a text or a key to an exercise, is usually necessary in order to allow students to help each other in this form of follow-up.

The *'pair-to-pair'* method means that each pair reports to another pair:

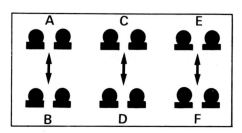

The *'rotating in pairs'* method means that, after first reporting 'pair-to-pair' (see above), the pairs rotate and meet new pairs. Thus:

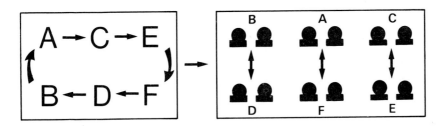

The same methods can naturally also be used with small groups instead of pairs.

3c. Follow-up in cross-reporting groups

This is the most complicated form of follow-up to organise but is often the most activating and rewarding.

With 20 students in a class who were working during the practice phase in 4 different groups, the cross-reporting groups are made so each new group contains one representative from each of the original groups:

Original groups   **Cross groups**

1	1	1	1		1	1	1	1
2	2	2	2		2	2	2	2
3	3	3	3		3	3	3	3
4	4	4	4		4	4	4	4
5	5	5	5		5	5	5	5

Thus, from 4 original groups with 5 students in each, we make 5 cross-groups with 4 students in each group.

> ● Organise cross-reporting groups for the following situations:
> **a.** 28 students working in 7 groups
> **b.** 15 students working in groups of 3
>
> ● Plan a group work and cross-reporting follow-up to suit one of your own classes

In the new cross-groups each representative reports in turn on the work done in the original group. In this way every student can compare results of work done in each of the original groups.

This method means **every** student must be active — both in the original group (making notes, writing answers, making summaries, etc.) and in the cross-group (reporting from the original group work and listening to others).

Cross-group reporting is an excellent method of following up any type of group practice such as:

- freer discussions
- vocabulary and grammar exercises
- problem-solving activities
- text-based activities

Arranging cross-reporting groups takes a little time. However, teachers need to remember two things. Firstly, if the teacher uses such groups regularly, students soon become familiar with how they work and very little time is spent on arranging the groups. Secondly, the short time which is "wasted" is soon paid for by a great increase in the amount of student activity such groups create.

- Which of the above forms of follow-up have you tried?

_____

_____

- What difficulties do you associate with each one?
  How could they be overcome?

_____

_____

- What role can the teacher play in the follow-up phase?

_____

_____

Correcting

"Teachers should be very careful about correcting students' mistakes".
"Students' mistakes should always be corrected".

- Which of the above statements do you *mostly* agree with?
- What sort of mistakes should be corrected?
- In what situations might it be best *not* to correct?
- *Who* should do the correcting?
- *How* should mistakes be corrected?

It is easy to assume the traditional role of the teacher as 'the authority', and constantly 'correct' mistakes. Often students themselves, particularly adults, expect this of the teacher. There are, however, situations where 'correcting' may do more harm than good. For example, interrupting a student during fluency practice or concentrating on individual errors in front of the whole class. This can create inhibitions in individual students and set standards of perfection that are difficult or impossible to live up to. Evidence also shows that constant correcting does not always lead to an improvement. On the other hand, the teacher has knowledge, skills and experience and the students need professional guidance. Much depends on *how* and *when* the correcting is done. The main considerations should be:

- to encourage and guide
- to be constructive
- to present correct models
- to concentrate on errors which interfere with understanding.

To reduce interruptions and corrections during an exercise or activity, the following steps could be taken:

before the practice

— provide some form of support (on the board or on paper)
— translate the first example together to check that everyone understands what to do
— work out a key or guidelines for the exercise.

during the practice

— the students use the key or guidelines to help or correct each other
— the teacher makes notes of mistakes to follow up *after* the practice
— the students make notes of uncertainties or difficulties to ask about after the practice.

after the practice

— concentrate on common mistakes which reveal a need for further explanation or practice, and those which may lead to misunderstanding
— as far as possible, avoid exposing individual errors in front of the whole class.

Fluency rather than 'correctness'

A willingness to use the language in a given situation can often be of greater importance for understanding and communication than grammatical correctness. It is therefore advisable to include freer forms of activities from a very early stage in language learning, even if this means that not everything is formally correct. Grammatical competence will normally develop as learning progresses. A half-developed language is an important stage in the process of language acquisition. An example of this could be *She not care* or *She don't care* before *She doesn't care.* This means the teacher should not be too concerned about letting certain mistakes, which do not interfere with communication, pass without being corrected. This is particularly true, for example, when students are working in groups or pairs for fluency practice. Many ideas for the communicative classroom are less effective if teachers worry too much about formal "correctness" too soon.

Openness and choice

In order for real communication to take place, language activities should allow for a certain amount of choice and openness. Exercises such as dialogues and role plays, for example, should therefore not be too strictly controlled, but should be capable of development in a variety of ways.

Summary

The most important ideas suggested by the approach and activities in this book are:

Student activity and co-operation
Emphasis on form rather than content
Reducing stress and anxiety
The importance of pair and group work
An emphasis on student/teacher co-operation
Encouraging personal involvement and creativity.

Activities

The activities are loosely divided into sections as follows:

Introductory Activities (1-5)

Activities in which different ways of beginning a course are presented. In addition, there is an activity which can be used as an introduction to the sound of the foreign language. All are suitable for use in the first lesson of a new course.

Vocabulary and Structure (6-21)

These activities practise word-building, spelling, vocabulary extension, phrase, structure and sentence construction. Many can be used for revision purposes. Most are game-orientated.

Dialogues (22-28)

All these activities are based on the use of dialogues. They range from the controlled to the free. At the beginning of a term or course it could be both practical and motivating to draw up a list together in class of situational dialogues to practise (eg. shopping, ordering tickets, telephone conversations, etc.). These can then be 'ticked off' as they are covered.

Text-based Activities (29-41)

These activities increase student involvement during the different phases of text work. A number of the activities use authentic text material. It is important that students have an opportunity of working with such material from the earliest stages of language learning. Working with "the real thing" encourages and motivates learners, shows the relevance of what they are learning, and prepares them for real language use, outside the classroom.

Listening Activities (42-49)

These activities cover such features as intonation, pronunciation and the sounds of the language, as well as understanding the content of what is heard.

Conversation, Discussion and Role-play (50-59)

The activities in this section range from the guided to the free, with the accent on the latter. Involvement and communication are the key aims of these activities. As with situational dialogues it can help to make a list of discussion topics and role-play situations together with the class at the beginning of a term.

Creative Activities (60-68)

This section contains activities designed to stimulate students' creative abilities in the foreign language. Although most of the activities in this book have an element of student creativity built into them, those contained in this section are based *primarily* on the input which the students themselves provide.

Miscellaneous (69-82)

This final section contains a mixed group of activities, varying widely in both content and aims. Some may stretch over a longer period of time, from one or two lessons to a whole term or more. The last activity in the section suggests, appropriately, a way of evaluating language studies.

Activities

Introductory Activities

1. Getting to know you
2. Who am I?
3. Find the right person
4. Pairs
5. What does it sound like?

Vocabulary and Structure

6. Oral clues
7. Odd men out
8. Similarities and differences
9. Sentence telepathy
10. Pass the note
11. Discover grammar
12. Consonant conundrums
13. Jumbled words and sentences
14. Shuffle
15. Grammar translations
16. Make your own grammar examples
17. Letter box
18. Word plaits
19. Picture drawing in groups
20. Respond to the situations
21. Classroom phrases

Dialogues

22. Cover-up dialogues
23. Core dialogues
24. Rub-out dialogues
25. Column Dialogues
26. Flow charts
27. Situational dialogues
28. Behaviour

Text-based Activities

29. Chain reading
30. Pause reading
31. Listen and fill in!
32. Re-create from memory
33. Key word summaries
34. Students' comprehension questions
35. Identify words and expressions
36. Reflecting on a text
37. Text substitutions
38. Fill the gaps
39. Cut and combine
40. Hard texts — easy tasks
41. Answer an ad

Listening Activities

42. Up or down?
43. Count the questions
44. Spot the mistakes
45. Identify attitudes
46. True or false?
47. Active listening
48. Listening in
49. Song lyrics

Conversation, Discussion and Role-play

50. What is it?
51. Guess the object
52. Mime interpretations
53. Seek advice
54. Double discussions
55. Guided role-play
56. Improvised role-plays
57. Discuss and report
58. Work visits
59. Debate

Creative Activities

60. Own dialogues
61. Construct-a-dialogue
62. Opinions and objections
63. Hooks
64. Rhyme time
65. Tell a joke
66. Continue the story
67. Associations
68. Letters to the editor

Miscellaneous

69. Shouting and whispering
70. The witness
71. Pictures from memory
72. Information gaps
73. Own information gaps
74. Puzzles
75. Our country
76. Make conversation
77. Visualisations
78. Help yourselves!
79. Team teaching
80. The block of flats
81. Projects
82. Evaluations

1. Getting to know you

Time : 20-30 minutes   **Level :** All

Language skills Interview-type activity with prepared questions centred around students' interests/family/home/work/language studies, etc.

Procedure

1. The whole class makes up questions in L1 to ask each other,eg:

> **What's your name?**
> **Where do you live?**
> **How do you come here?**
> **What's your favourite hobby? etc.**

Each question is translated with the teacher's help and written on the board.

2. Students work in pairs and take turns to ask and answer the questions.

3. Continue the activity by making new pairs.

Comments It is important to note that in this activity the *students them-selves* make up the questions. A suitable activity to "break the ice" with a new class and to get to know one another. At beginners' level the activity may be conducted entirely in L1; at more advanced levels, in L2. The principal objective is that students meet each other and relax; this is more important than the language used at this stage. With this in mind teachers must not correct mistakes or "interfere" unless encouraged to do so by participants themselves. For post-beginners, extra whole-class practice of question and answer models in L2 may be advisable prior to pair-work. Allow time for follow-up of common difficulties and points of general interest.

"Now let's see—who don't you know?"

2. Who am I?

Time : 25-40 minutes   **Level :** Intermediate, Advanced

Language skills Talking about yourself — likes and dislikes, interests, desires, etc. Interviewing other people and asking follow-up questions.

Procedure

1. The teacher writes the following or similar sentences in L2 on the board or on paper:

    1. **A country I would like to visit**
    2. **The last book I read**
    3. **My favourite singer/group/type of music**
    4. **Where I spent my last holiday**
    5. **Something I like doing**
    6. **My favourite food or dish**
    7. **A film I remember**
    8. **Something I dislike**
    9. **A person I admire**
    10. **Something I would like to do**

2. Students have a maximum of 10 minutes to write their own answers to as many as possible of the points. It is often enough to write single word answers. These should be written on a separate piece of paper.

3. Divide the class into groups of 3 or 4 students. The students in each group then talk to one another in L2, using as a basis the sentences on the board and their own papers.

4. After the group conversations the papers are collected and then redistributed at random. Each student reads what is written on the new piece of paper he/she has received. The rest of the class try to say who has written it.

Comments This activity gives the students an opportunity to get to know one another and use the foreign language to talk about themselves. In addition the teacher gets to know something about the new students - their interests, their ability in the target language and their confidence in using it. Students prepare quietly so the embarrassment of being asked to answer immediately is avoided.

---

3. Find the right person

Time : about 20 minutes   **Level :** All except beginners

Language skills Making questions, giving simple information about your-self, simple responses — *Yes I am/can/do,* etc. Could be useful to teach an expression such as *I'm afraid not* and encourage students to use it during the practice.

Procedure

1. The teacher prepares a set of cards each containing an idea such as the following in L2:

    Someone who has been to Scotland.
    Someone who hates using the telephone.
    Someone who prefers tea to coffee.
    Someone whose favourite sport is tennis.
    Someone who likes Italian food.
    Someone with at least four brothers and sisters.
    Someone who can't ride a bike.
    Someone who remembers their great grandmother.
    Someone who can speak German.
    Someone whose birthday is in June.

2. Each student is given a card. The students then stand up, walk around the room and try to find somebody in the group who fits the descrip-tion on their card. It is sometimes a good idea to help students first by giving one or two sentences in L2 on the board which show them how to turn the information on their card into questions:

    Can you speak German?
    Is your birthday in June?
    Do you like Italian food?

Comments This activity again de-focusses — the emphasis of the activity is on finding the right person, not on the language used. The activity can be made more difficult by adding the extra condition that each partner of a pair must "fit" with the sentences on the other partner's card.

4. Pairs

Time : 15-20 minutes   **Level :** All

Language skills The language of the examples themselves — which may be small groups of sentences (for example, in the set below, question forms, some tags, and important conversational phrases). In addition, students should also use language for meeting each other, saying that they do/do not believe that they belong together etc.

Procedure

1. The teacher prepares a set of sentences and divides each sentence into parts (see example below). The half sentences are neatly written or typed on cards, or prepared on a piece of paper and cut into strips. Use one strip for each student.

2. Students stand up, and walk around the room looking for "their other half". If they think they have found a partner they stay together, but they must move if necessary so that every student may find a partner. In the examples below, for example, it is possible to make the pair *What are you looking for?* but it is not possible to make* *Who are you doing?* If the people with *What are you . . .* and *. . . looking for?* join, they will have to split up again so that the students with *Who are you . . .* and *. . . doing?* can find partners.

3. The students must be told that the activity is over only when *everyone* has found the correct partner. Teachers should make the sentences so that there is only *one* possible solution where *everybody* has a partner.

Comments This activity is de-focused as a language teaching activity, even though the focus is on sentences in L2. There is no pressure on students to produce new and correct sentences themselves. The emphasis of the activity is not on the language, but on "looking for your partner". Students consider the possibility of a very wide number of sentences, all of which should be natural expressions. Without much conscious effort, students examine a lot of language which is useful for them. Some parts of this activity are new — using language items as the basis of an ice-breaker at the beginning of a course. *Starting* a course with something that emphasises both language *and* a relaxed social atmosphere in the classroom. The emphasis on working *together* from the first moments of a course.

It is important to notice that the sets of examples are not just the first ten sentences that come into the teacher's head. The following points are important:

Activities

a. It is helpful to make *groups* of sentences, which may cause confusion at first but which show a clear difference when students look carefully at them, e.g. the question examples at the beginning of the set below.

b. It helps to have some standard phrases which students should already know, but which are perhaps divided in an unusual place:
How do. . .you do.   That's quite . . .all right.

It helps the teacher to make up group practices if the examples contain two different kinds of clues, structural *(There's a...isn't there)* and semantic *(Who are you...looking for?).*

Example sentences

What are you	doing?
Where	are you going?
Who are you	looking for?
When are you	going?
How do	you do.
Have a	good trip!
Not	at all!
What a	wonderful surprise!
What an	awful shock!
That's quite	all right.
There's a baker's in Green Street	isn't there?
We've met	before, haven't we?
You didn't do it	did you?
It's	a lovely day.
There's	none left.

(You may photocopy these examples to use with your classes)

Variation This may also be done using two-line dialogues, pairing "question" and response, for example:

Thanks for your help.	Don't mention it.
Could you give me a hand, please.	Certainly.
When are you leaving?	In a moment.
Do you mind if we say half past?	No, not at all.

Again the whole set of sentences should be chosen so that there is only one solution.

5. What does it sound like?

Time : 10-15 minutes   **Level :** Beginners

Language skills A first free association with the sound of the L2.

Procedure

1. Play a recording, no longer than a minute or so, in the foreign language (L2) without any preparation.

2. Discuss in L1, first in pairs and then in the whole class, what it sounded like. Ask students for their general impression, associations, etc.

3. Play the recording a second time and ask the students to give impressions of more specific features of the language, eg. characteristic sounds, softness/hardness, speed of delivery, pitch of voice, rhythm and intonation, etc.

4. Discuss again, first in pairs then in the whole class.

Comments Suitable activity to use in the first lesson with a new language. The teacher should be prepared to counter possible negative comments from the students about the way the foreign language sounded. This is often best done by being specific (point 3 above), and by comparing with other languages known to the class — in particular the sound of their own language to people for whom it is a foreign language.

It is helpful to recognize that students do have prejudices about the language they are learning (or are going to learn) and these are not always helpful. Discussing them openly is an effective way of relaxing students and making them more "open" to the new language.

---

6. Oral cues

Time : about 5 minutes   **Level :** All

Language skills Comprehension of items out of context and ability to insert quickly and correctly in a given context.

Procedure

1. Teacher writes a sentence in L2 on the board for example:

    "I like peaches and cream"

2. Students read sentence aloud in chorus.

3. Teacher gives an oral cue for a substitute, for example:

    "Strawberries"

4. One student repeats the original sentence, making the substitute as appropriate:

    "I like strawberries and cream"

5. The new sentence is then repeated by the whole class.

6. Teacher gives a new oral cue such as: *Ice-cream, apple pie, custard, don't like, he,* etc.For each new cue the teacher asks another student to produce the new sentence.

Comments The teacher could write the cues, one by one, on the board as an aid to memory. The original sentence thus undergoes a progressive transformation. A brisk pace is best for this activity.

Variation When students are familiar with this activity it could be done in pairs with one in each pair having a written copy of the original sentence and a list of cues.

7. Odd men out

Time : 5-10 minutes   **Level :** All

Language skills Connections between words and explaining reasons.

Procedure

1. The teacher writes a list of four words on the board, For example:

    SEA   CLOUD   ICE   RAIN

    WALK   RUN   JUMP   GALLOP

2. Each student tries to make a group of three words that belong together. The fourth word is the 'odd man out'. The important point is that *there is no 'correct' answer.* In each group of words there should be at least two possible 'odd men out'.

3. In whole class — students say which word they have chosen as 'odd man out' and give reasons.

4. Continue with new groups of words. Work first individually, then in pairs or small groups to compare.

Comments In the conventional puzzle form of this activity there is only one correct answer. This alternative gives more opportunity for creative thinking and language practice. It also avoids the problem of 'right' or 'wrong' answers which can worry and demotivate some students.

The sets of examples should be made so that they may be grouped in at least two different ways. Usually this means two ways of grouping by *meaning:*

Hand, eye, nose, ear, cheek.

Hand is not part of the face. We do not have two *noses.*

It is also possible to make groups in quite different ways. For example, in the set given above *(walk, run, jump, gallop)* only *run* has an irregular past tense form. Here are some alternative ways of making groups:

1. Go, snow, *now,* low (pronunciation).
2. Put, set, *make,* cost (grammar — types of irregular verb).
3. Sock, shoe, *shirt,* trousers (grammar — *a pair of).*
4. Possible, perfect, polite, *popular* (grammar — opposite *im-).*
5. Played, listened, smiled, *walked* (pronunciation of *-ed).*
6. Calm, knowledge, *silent,* autumn (silent letters).
7. Man, woman, child, *boy* (irregular plural).
8. Church, which, *machine,* choose (pronunciation *ch).*

Students should be encouraged to group examples in any way they like, providing they can give a reason for their choice of the odd man out.

8. Similarities and differences

Time : 5-10 minutes   **Level :** Intermediate, Advanced

Language skills Comparisons. Constructions using words/phrases such as *both, only one, the....has/is, but the....hasn't/isn't,* etc.

Procedure

1. The teacher writes two words on the board. For example:

   COW   DOG

2. Students try to find as many features as possible that they have in common — the *similarities* (animals; have four legs; tame, etc.). They then suggest all the *differences* they can think of (the cow has horns, but not the dog; only the cow produces food for humans; the dog can be a house pet; the cow is bigger than the dog, etc.)

3. Continue with new pairs of words, working first in pairs, then checking in the whole class.

Comments Suitable as short activity to start or finish a lesson. Encourages divergent thinking — new ways of seeing familiar objects. Teachers could give sentence patterns at lower level, but variety of sentence construction should be encouraged at higher levels.

The words may be chosen so that the activity is suitable for different ages or different levels of ability in the L2. Pairs of nouns are often easiest; verbs and adjectives more difficult, both linguistically and conceptually. The 'level' should challenge students but not frighten them!

The words may be of different kinds, but usually the same grammatical group (nouns, verbs, and adjectives). Here are some examples:

meal	**snack**	**banana**	**strawberry**
friend	**acquaintance**	**eye**	**ear**
beautiful	**attractive**	**house**	**flat**
important	**valuable**	**walk**	**run**
see	**watch**	**smile**	**laugh**

9. Sentence telepathy

Time : 5-10 minutes   **Level :** All

Language skillls Identifying grammatical categories and examples of them; at higher levels, collocations.

Procedure

1. The teacher thinks up a short, simple sentence in L2 and draws a line on the board to represent each word in the sentence:

　　　____　　　_____　　　_____　　　__ __　　　_____
　　　(mio)　　　(fratello)　　　(abita)　　　(in)　　　(America)

It is important to use a high proportion of 'structural', rather than 'content' words, if the activity is to be effective.

2. The teacher says that (s)he will try to communicate the sentence to the class "by telepathy". The students should "concentrate hard" and offer suggestions, beginning with the first word. It helps if students first establish what kind of word it is — verb? adjective? pronoun? etc.

3. Each time a correct word is said, the teacher writes it in place of the appropriate line on the board, until the sentence is complete.

Comments Suitable as a short activity at the beginning or end of lesson. Especially popular with younger students. Encouraging students to guess, and explore *possible* sentences instead of searching for a 'right' answer. The *process* of the activity is more important than the result. When the first word has been established the guesses become easier because they are more informed, and systematic. Even advanced classes will enjoy the activity if sentences using appropriate colloquial or collocational phrases are included, such as:

> *I still see her every now and then.*

> *Shall we call it a day?*

10. Pass the note

Time : 5-15 minutes   **Level :** All, especially intermediate

Language skills Translation into L1 or L2 of words, phrases or sentences. Vocabulary and structure revision.

Procedure

1. Form groups. Within each group each student writes on a piece of paper words, fixed expressions or sentences in L2. The L1 equivalent is then written on the reverse side of each piece of paper.

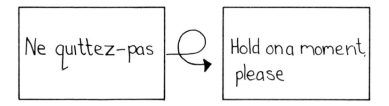

2. The notes are then passed around within each group, either side face-up. Each person tries to translate the notes received into L1 or L2 as the case may be. Check afterwards by turning the note over.

3. Continue to pass the notes around in the group.

Comments Simple to organize. This activity is best conducted at a lively speed. May be restricted to a certain topic or area of vocabulary for revision purposes. If unrestricted, the preparation phase may take longer, but improves the practice. It is helpful to remind students that they can write whole expressions that they have learned as well as single words or 'new' sentences that they have invented.

11. Discover grammar

Time : 10-15 minutes   **Level :** All, particularly elementary, intermediate

Language skills Observation and discovery of structural patterns; deduction of descriptive grammatical rules.

Procedure

1. The teacher distributes a text in which examples of a certain grammatical feature occur. The students are asked to find a pattern, relationship or rule. For example:

> -¿ Ellos son suecos?
> - No. Él es alemán y ella es danés.
> -¿ Y tú eres tambien danés?
> - No. Yo soy sueca!

Fill in the Spanish personal pronouns:

I	_____	we	nosotros
you	_____	you	vosotros
he	_____	they	_____
she	_____		

2. Work in pairs to solve the task and find a pattern or formulate a rule.

3. Check afterwards in a grammar book or with the teacher.

Comments This activity is based on the principle that people are more likely to learn and remember something they have worked out for themselves. It is an alternative to the conventional method in which the teacher gives the rule and the students listen, when everyone *seems* involved, but much is often mis-heard and mis-understood without the teacher knowing. The process of observation, making guesses, correcting etc. is all part of the learning activity. It means students are constantly involved.

12. Consonant conundrums

Time : 10-15 minutes   **Level :** All

Language skills Spelling and pronunciation, with focus on consonants and groups of consonants, common combinations in the language (e.g. in English, *str-, sp-, thr-.)* Decoding a partly legible message. Understanding of word order.

Procedure

1. The teacher writes a simple sentence on the board but omits all the vowels:
    WRSNDSHRMD (German)
    WHTTMSTPLS? (English)

2. The students try to solve the conundrum by supplying the vowels. (answers: *Wir sind sehr müde; What time is it, please?)*

3. Continue in pairs. Each pair makes a new example to circulate among the other pairs.

Comments This activity also trains skills of association from a visual stimulus in telegraphic or abbreviated forms.

It is very much easier if the word breaks and missing letters spaces are shown:

TH—R—   W—S   —   M—N   —N   TH—   G—RD—N.
It is much more of a puzzle if the word breaks are not shown:

H—V—Y——B— —NT—L—ND—NB—F—R—?

And if you are not careful, problems can be so difficult that they do not help students, only annoy them! Unless you want a *very* difficult example, avoid words with groups of vowels *(our, year),* words which are *only* vowels *(a,I)* or a lot of words beginning with vowels *(is, it, or).*

If you want to see how difficult the examples *can* be, try these two (English) examples. Both are quite simple natural sentences:

FSHRLLSKHR.

WWNTNDRMBRLLS.

(answers on page 125)
Remember, the examples you make must *help* students to guess, not trick them. Of course the examples are much easier if they use words and structures students have met and studied recently.

13. Jumbled words and sentences

Time : 10-20 minutes   **Level :** All

Language skills Spelling. Agreement and verb forms. Word order and sentence formation.

Procedure

1. The teacher writes letters and words, jumbled up, on the board.

    (French)

2. The students first try to make a word in each block and then to sort the words into a sentence. (Example: *Elles sont belles*)

3. Continue in pairs. Each pair makes up a new example. Pass the examples around amongst the other pairs.

Comments A useful activity to practise difficulties such as adjectival agreement in, for example, French, word order and syntax. Can give rise to discussion on semantic variations. The activity may be restricted to include extracts from a known text, or to have a limited number of words or even to contain a specific structure pattern. The de-focusing of the game can actually help students look more effectively at the details of the structure, with more chance of subconscious acquisition.

14. Shuffle

Time : 10-20 minutes   **Level :** Intermediate, Advanced

Language skills Vocabulary revision, word order and sentence construction. At lower levels it applies particularly to the position of adverbs and adverb phrases. At higher levels also to 'comments' such as *apparently, frankly, actually, as a matter of fact.*

Procedure

1. A number of sentences are given to the students on the board or on paper. Certain words or phrases are left out of the sentences. These are written in random order to the side, eg:

I don't like potatoes	by bus
He goes to school in the morning	yesterday
The train for Paris left at 7 o'clock	at all

2. The students, working alone or in pairs, try to put the words/phrases in the correct places.

3. Check the results pair-to-pair and then in the whole class.

4. Group work: students make similar examples of their own which they then exchange with other groups.

Comments This activity bridges the gap between reading and writing skills. Focuses on the neglected skill of word order.

Three points may be emphasised:
a. Pressure on students to "be right" is reduced because they are only concentrating on order, not constructing correct sentences themselves.

b. The pair work activity also reduces tension and increases student involvement.

c. Because students examine different possibilities without the pressure of creating correct sentences from nothing, they are more likely to retain the important language teaching element of the activity.

15. Grammar translations

Time : 15-25 minutes   **Level :** Intermediate, Advanced

Language skills Translation of sentences illustrating specific points of grammar, perhaps particularly those which regularly cause interference mistakes.

Procedure

1. Work individually. Each student chooses some sentences illustrating a specific grammar point from a grammar book. Translate these sentences into L1 on a separate piece of paper.

2. Work in pairs. Exchange papers and translate each other's sentences back into L2.

3. Check the correct versions in the grammar book.

Comments The final stage of translating back into L2 focuses on the grammar point in question. The students may choose easier or more difficult examples.

16. Make your own grammar examples

Time : 15-20 minutes   **Level :** Intermediate. Advanced

Language skills Understanding of grammatical patterns. Creative use of such understanding.

Procedure

1. Study a grammatical rule, structure or pattern, using, for example, the discovery method, activity 11.

2. Put aside the grammar book. Students work in pairs and try together to make their own examples in L2 to illustrate the point.

3. Present the various examples in the whole class and discuss possible errors and how the rule was illustrated.

Comments By making up examples of their own the teacher can see whether the students have assimilated the grammar point in question. The more relaxed atmosphere of discussing students' own examples makes it easier for the teacher to deal with possible misunderstandings. Although this approach may take a little longer initially than the conventional "teacher - explaining", it is much more likely to mean students really understand, internalise and retain. The emphasis, as with all activities in this book, is on good language *learning,* as opposed to teaching! The activity makes "grammar" a subject of discussion and exploration, by using the students' own examples.

17. Letter box

Time : 20-30 minutes   **Level :** All

Language skills Searching for vocabulary from the secret stock of words in your head; identifying common sound patterns of the language.

Procedure

1. Take a 9-letter word in L2. Jumble the letters and then arrange them in a box (see example):

(Italian)

(Answer: APERITIVO)

2. Students make as many L2 words as possible, including the full 9-letter word, from the given letters. Each letter can only be used once in each word. Set a time limit of, say, 10 minutes.

3. Form small groups. Each group makes a combined list from the individual ones in that group.

4. Check in the whole class. One group starts, after which others, in turn, add new words not previously mentioned.

5. The teacher can write up new or difficult words on the board.

6. Follow up with vocabulary exercises on the words written on the board. eg.
    — **Which word means. . .?**
    — **What words can you build from. . .?**
    — **What is the opposite of. . .?**
    — **Make up a sentence with the word. . .?**
    — **Where do you find a. . .?**

7. Students choose their own jumbled words, perhaps with the help of a dictionary, and circulate them in the class, either in the same lesson or on a later occasion.

Comments A good activity for training spelling and for identifying groups of letters that make up common word stems, suffixes and prefixes. Dictionaries may be used to check words suggested. Words of different lengths may be used for variation.

English, for example, has many words with these groups:

it:	bit, hit, lit
eat:	beat, heat, neat, seat, treat
ate:	date, gate, hate, late, rate
ight:	light, night, sight
en:	hen, when, pen, men, ten

Many English words end in *-er, -est, -ed*

The nine letter word chosen should 'help' students by containing letters to make some of the common combinations: Here are a few nine letter words:

telephone	**beautiful**	**September**
breakfast	**recognise**	**chocolate**
dangerous	**different**	**newspaper**

---

18. Word plaits

Time : 20-30 minutes   **Level :** Elementary, Intermediate

Language skills Spelling, vocabulary; defining; opposites; synonyms.

Procedure
1. Each student constructs a word plait similar to the example below:

            Clues: Solution:

Clues are given to the words across. The aim is to solve the puzzle and find the 'down' word.

2. Make copies of all the word plaits and staple together to make a little puzzle book.

3. Students work individually to solve the puzzles, then compare with each other.

Comments Suitable as vocabulary revision exercise at all levels of language learning. The difficulty of the clues can vary according to the level. They may be illustrations (see example), L1 translations or:

a synonym	*big*	Answer: *enormous*
an antonym	*not old*	Answer: *young*
"fill-the-gap"	"_____ *me, can you*	
	change a pound?"	Answer: *excuse*
whole sentence	A place where scientific experi-	
	ments are done.	Answer: *laboratory*

Students may be encouraged to use dictionaries to write their clues. It is important to remember that the object of an activity like this is to encourage the *subconscious* use of language skills.

19. Picture drawing in groups

Time : about 15 minutes **Level :** All, particularly elementary

Language skills Vocabulary of parts of the body. Writing descriptions of people.

Procedure

1. The class is divided into groups of 4-6 students. Each group is given a large piece of blank paper or a section of the board to work on. The task is for each group to draw a picture of a person, each student drawing one part of the body at a time. The other students in the group name that part as it is being drawn.

2. When the drawings are complete, the groups move on to another group's drawing and together write a description of the figure.

Comments This activity can be done at different levels of proficiency. An amusing revision of the language and skills involved. Teacher should act as resource when students cannot supply the relevant words.

Other subjects for group drawings are:
        a car, a house, furniture,
        a landscape view, a street scene, a face.

Again the activity has a serious learning purpose: formal language learning is de-focused, but all students can contribute in a relaxed atmosphere.

20. Respond to the situation

Time : 20-30 minutes   **Level :** Intermediate, Advanced

Language skills Revision and practice of idioms and "situational phrases" in context.

Procedure

1. Whole class — make a list together, in L1, of typical situations in which a set response is called for, such as:

    What do I say when someone. . .
        — greets me
        — introduces himself to me
        — misunderstands me
        — speaks too fast for me
        — says something rude to me
        — asks me the way
        — asks me to help, but I can't

2. Work in pairs. Using textbooks and dictionaries or grammar books, if necessary, write down suitable expressions in L2 for each situation.

3. Write short dialogues, using the expressions.

4. Practise the dialogue in pairs.

5. Follow up, in the whole class or pair-to-pair by enacting situations, each pair taking turns to act a scene.

Comments Idiomatic and situational phrases need considerable practice in the foreign language if they are to become a natural and automatic part of the student's repertoire. Short, communicative "sketches" enacted in pairs are more likely to be remembered than conventional learning of isolated phrases from the textbook.

21. Classroom phrases

Time : about 30 minutes   **Level :** Elementary, Intermediate

Language skills Translation of phrases into L2 with the help of wordlists and dictionaries. Imperatives and questions in the classroom context.

Procedure

1. Make a list together in L1 of common phrases used in the classroom:

Take out your books. . .	**Do you understand?**
Turn to page. . .	**Are there any questions?**
Close your books.	**What does . . . mean?**
Open your books.	**What is. . . in German/English, etc.?**
Write on the board.	**How do you spell . . .?**
Look up. . .in the wordlist	**Form pairs/groups of three.**
/dictionary.	**It is your turn to read/ask/answer.**
Answer question. . .	**Ask . . . what s/he thinks.**

2. In small groups work together with the help of wordlists and dictionaries to translate the list into L2. Everyone takes notes.

3. Compare notes afterwards in new cross-reporting groups. Agree in each group on the best translation for each phrase.

4. Practise the phrases in the groups, by taking turns to be the "teacher". The others in the group carry out the instructions or answer the questions.

Comments Focuses attention on language used in the learning situation. Although this language is usually "passive" (teacher instructions), this activity can encourage the use of L2 in the management of the language lesson. Some of the phrases can be actively student-orientated. *(How do you spell. . .? What does. . .mean?* etc.) Some phrases useful for the learner outside the classroom *(Sorry? I'm afraid I don't understand.)* also occur and can be practised.

22. Cover-up dialogues

Time : 3-10 minutes   **Level :** Elementary, Intermediate

Language skills Intensive vocabulary and structure practice.

Procedure

1. Practise a dialogue by repeating in chorus a few times after the teacher or the tape. Make sure the language content is fully understood.

2. Pairwork — One in each pair covers over part of the dialogue, step by step, with a piece of paper, for example:

	Step 2	**Step 1**
Garçon:	**Qu'est-ce que vous voulez?**	
Jean:	**Je veux du lait bien frais.**	
Garçon:	**Il n'y a pas de lait...**	
Jean:	**Alors, donnez-moi de la bière.**	

3. Cover over more and more of the dialogue and repeat until students can do the whole dialogue without help from the text.

Comments A good example of an activity based on the principle of limiting or reducing the amount of help given by the text. Note that it is better if each response in the dialogue covers *one written line* only.

23. Core dialogues

Time : 5-10 minutes   **Level :** Elementary, Intermediate

Language skills Intensive practice of word groups in a natural context. Word groups to focus on may be:

— nouns, verbs, adjectives, adverbs, prepositions, (grammatical groups)
— phrases, question forms, vocabulary items (situation or topic-related)

Procedure

1. The teacher writes an example dialogue in L2 on the board:

    Cameriere: Cosa desidera da bere?
    Cliente: Un bicchiera di. . .

2. The teacher puts a list of substitutions on the board in L1.

    1. milk
    2. orange juice
    3. mineral water
    4. wine

    Students write the L2 translations (the key) on a piece of paper, which can be put aside during the activity.

3. Pairs. One is the "waiter", the other a "guest". The "waiter" begins with his line and the "guest" answers by inserting the first substitute word on the board. Both can check that the correct translation was used by looking at the key.

4. Change roles after all the substitute words have been practised by the "guest".

Comments An effective way of practising language in context with high student activity.

The difficulty may be varied by giving students a key, a jumbled key (the correct words or phrases in the wrong order), or no key.

Access to a key allows independence and co-operation in the pair work. If this type of activity is unfamiliar, demonstrate first with a few exchanges from the dialogue in the whole class before doing the pair work.

Each pair may work at own pace, with the teacher available to help where needed. Those who finish early may repeat the activity, this time by trying to "say their lines" without looking at the example dialogue.

Finally, the technique can be made more student-centred by letting the students, in groups, make up their own word-groups. Copy down the lists for future use. These can then be the basis for constructing new core dialogues by the students themselves.

The core dialogue may also be grammatical or situational as with the substitutions below:

Grammar — verbs in past tense	**Situational — giving directions**
A Comment êtes-vous venu ici?	**A Wie kommen wir zum Bahnhof, bitte?**
B Aujourd'hui. . .	**B . . und dann sehen Sie den Bahnhof.**
Substitutions	Substitutions
1. I ran	1. Go straight on
2. I came by bus	2. Turn left
3. I walked	3. Turn right
4. I cycled	4. Go to the square
5. I drove	5. Take the first turning on the right

24. Rub-out dialogues

Time : 5-10 minutes   **Level :** Elementary, Intermediate

Language skills Memorisation of important lexical or structural items in a dialogue context.

Procedure

1. Teacher writes a short dialogue on the board.

2. Choral repetition.

3. The teacher rubs out some words or phrases replacing each word with a line.

4. Pairs repeat the dialogue filling in the missing items.

5. Continue with the teacher rubbing out more and more until only gaps are left on the board.

Comments This should be carried out at quite a brisk tempo, teacher-controlled. Interest and participation is likely to increase as more and more of the original is successively rubbed out. The task may be made easier or more difficult by the order in which words are rubbed out as these first steps show:

> It's quite all right.
> It's quite all_____ (Easy)
> It's _____ all right. (More difficult)
> It's _____ right.   (Still more difficult)

Similary, if students have not met the expression *for a living* before and it is introduced in
What do you do for a living?
there are three alternative ways of rubbing out:

What do you do____ __ _____ ?	(remove the new part as quickly as possible so students concentrate on it all the time)
What do _____ ___ for a living? *____ ____ ____ ____ for a living?*	(remove it last, so students see the new part as long as possible)
What do you do _____ a living?	(remove the new item bit by bit)

Try different methods on different occasions to maintain interest, and help students' concentration.

Variation A student may come to the board and do the rubbing out. This increases participation but is less controlled as the student may rub out items which make the activity much more difficult. At the same time the positive contribution of letting a student be "in control" is important.

25. Column dialogues

Time : 5-10 minutes   **Level :** Elementary, Intermediate

Language skills Intensive practice of structure or situational phrases. Intensive listening practice.

Procedure

1. Rewrite a dialogue in column form, eg:

Ingrid	Anna
Wo bist du gewesen? Was hast du da gemacht? Etc.	In Berlin Ich habe Freunde besucht Etc.

2. Work in pairs. Begin by covering over, first, your partner's lines and then, later, your own lines with a piece of paper.

3. Change roles and repeat the procedure.

Comments Covering over your partner's lines encourages active listening, whereas covering over your own lines encourages concentration and recall.

52

Activities

26. Flow charts

Time : 10-20 minutes   **Level :** Mostly Intermediate

Language skills Practice of specific functions such as complaining, apologising, refusing, accepting, etc; important conversation phrases *(please, I'm afraid,* etc.), links *(Really? Have you?)* and fillers *(a kind of, do you see what I mean);* active listening.

Procedure

1. The teacher makes up a chart/diagram in L1 based on a situation that has been practised earlier (eg. making an offer, accepting or refusing).

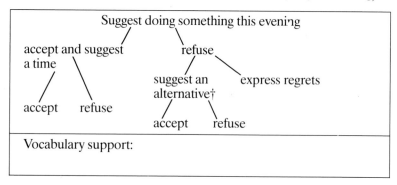

2. Work in pairs, using the chart to make up a number of short dialogues, following different paths through the chart.

3. Progress from oral to written practice.

Comments Many textbooks now contain *fixed* situational or functional dialogues. The advantage of this activity is the choice that each student has. This means students need to listen carefully and make appropriate responses, just as in a real conversation.
The branches of the chart are usually based on alternative, positive/negative responses, but can also mean the 'initiator' changes, as in the example above, at † in the diagram.

27. Situational dialogues

Time : 20-40 minutes   **Level :** Intermediate

Language skills Intensive practice of situational phrases. Vocabulary revision. Use of important interactional language *(excuse me; please)*, stress and intonation.

Procedure

1. Form pairs. Each pair decides on a typical tourist situation such as "trying on and buying a sweater" or "buying railway tickets".

2. With the help of dictionaries, each pair works together to make a list of words and phrases that might normally occur in that situation.

3. Using the lists as a basis each pair then writes a dialogue for the situation.

4. In the whole class, students and teacher comment on the dialogues, adding phrases, correcting important errors or omissions.

5. Practise the dialogues first in pairs, then act out to the rest of the class.

6. Exchange papers and practise one another's dialogues.

Comments Allowing students to create their own dialogues generates more interest and creates a greater variety of material for the class to use in step 6.

---

28. Behaviour

Time : 20-30 minutes   **Level :** Advanced

Language skills Vocabulary and functional expressions associated with various social situations.

Procedure

1. Form small groups. Discuss, in L1 or L2, differences in behaviour between people in the home country and those in the country/countries whose language is being studied. Discussion may focus on, for example:

   — The use of different 'you' forms
     (*tu-vous* French, *du-Sie* German, *tu-Lei* Italian)
   — The use of Christian v Surname
   — Situations where people shake hands
   — The use of gestures
   — How people answer the phone
   — What people say/do when visiting friends
   — What is acceptable/unacceptable behaviour when eating
   — Relationships between young people and adults
   — Bringing up children

2. Work in pairs. Choose one of the examples listed. Write down expressions that you think are appropriate in these circumstances. If necessary, use dictionaries or ask the teacher.

3. Make up a short dialogue using some of the expressions. It is best to limit the dialogue to 5 or 6 lines.

4. Practise the dialogues in pairs.

5. When all pairs are ready, act out the dialogues for one another in the whole class or by rotating in pairs.

Comments This activity focuses attention on cultural differences and how they affect language. The verbal exchanges should be accompanied by appropriate behaviour such as hand-shaking, use of gestures and so on. Learning is more likely to be reinforced if the situations simulate real ones as closely as possible and the students invest more of themselves in the activity. Because such language and discussion are often not part of a conventional language course, the activity may be useful for quite advanced learners, for whom the discussion may be new.

29. Chain reading

Time : 2-5 minutes   **Level :** Elementary, Intermediate

Language skills Active listening to a text reading. Reading aloud.

Procedure

1. One student begins reading a text. The others follow in their books.

2. The reader suddenly stops, even in the middle of a word or phrase, and says the name of another student who continues the reading.

3. Continue until the text is completed or all students have had a turn at reading.

Comments Since reading aloud is a demanding task in itself, this is best done with a prepared text to minimise reading or pronunciation errors. The surprise element encourages a more active participation from all students and the transfer of control from the teacher to the students in naming the next reader also adds to the enjoyment and degree of activity.
It is possible for the teacher, too, to be 'in the game' so a student may call the teacher's name for the next turn. This activity turns reading into an active listening exercise, involving *all* students, *all* the time.

30. Pause reading

Time : 5-10 minutes   **Level :** Elementary, Intermediate

Language skills Active listening. Contextual guessing or recall.

Procedure

1. The teacher, or a student, reads from a known text, the others listen, books shut.

2. Sudden pauses are made in the reading and students attempt to supply the words or phrases that immediately follow in the text by offering verbal suggestions.

Comments Demands on attention and aural comprehension are increased compared with the previous activity (Chain reading). Alternatives to the text version should be accepted so long as they are appropriate to the context.

Variations The activity may also be done in pairs or small groups with one student in each pair or group reading from the text. The same activity may be conducted with an *unknown* text, which places greater demands on the skill of aural comprehension and contextual guessing. It encourages students to find *possible,* not "the correct", answers.

31. Listen and fill in!

Time : 10-15 minutes   **Level :** Elementary, Intermediate

Language skills Accurate, intensive listening; contextual comprehension; spelling.

Procedure

1. A text with omitted words or phrases is copied and a copy given to each student.

2. Form groups. One student in each group reads out the original complete text, and the others write in the missing words or phrases.

3. Afterwards each student compares his or her own text with the original.

Comments A way of varying dictation so that students are involved.

32. Recreate from memory

Time : 5-10 minutes   **Level :** All

Language skills Oral reproduction of information contained in a text. Listening or reading comprehension.

Procedure

1. All students read a text, or listen to a reading of the text.

2. Afterwards the teacher asks just one question: *What do you remember from the text?* The students then volunteer information as it comes to them, thus gradually recreating the basic contents of the passage.

Comments A highly activating activity. Each successive contribution produces a chain reaction of new memories and associations. Even "weaker" students find it easier to participate than with a more conventional form of text comprehension exercise.

33. Key word summaries

Time : 15 minutes or more   **Level :** All

Language skills General comprehension. Oral reproduction — intensive text; comprehension and oral summarising — extensive text.

Procedure

1. Form groups. Each group selects some key words of a known text, eg:

> **Elke und Petra sind <u>Freundinnen</u>. Heute wollen sie zusammen <u>einkaufen</u>. Sie nehmen den <u>Bus</u>.**

These key words are to form the basis for retelling the text.

2. The key words are written down on a separate piece of paper. Someone in the group then tries to make an oral summary of the text, using only the key words. The others in the group can provide support from the text, if necessary. Take turns in making the summary.

3. Exchange summaries with another group and repeat the procedure.

Comments This activity may be used:
>   — as an extension phase of textwork
>   — for revision of a text previously studied
>   — with an extensive text, such as a newspaper article at more
>   advanced levels.

This can be quite a demanding activity involving comprehension, selection of important facts (key words) and then summarising.

34. Students' comprehension questions

Time : 10-15 minutes   **Level :** Elementary, Intermediate

Language skills Question forms. Text comprehension.

Procedure

1. Each student makes up 3 questions on a known text, and writes them down.

2. Work in small groups. Each student, in turn, asks all his or her questions; the others answer, with or without the text. The one who is asking the questions can look at the text and check if the answers are correct.

Comments Questions can produce different types of answer, ranging from a simple *"Yes/No"*, to reproduction of information from the text, or even interpretation or extension of the content of the text. Each student may form either very easy-to-answer or more complex questions — allowing for a more individualised teaching style.

Letting students make comprehension questions is more involving, more likely to show mis-understandings (it's more difficult to make questions about the text than to answer them!) It also ensures students practise both question and statement forms — in much traditional teaching the *teacher* makes all the question forms, while in real life students are as likely to need question forms as statements.

35. Identify words and expressions

Time : 10-15 minutes   **Level** : Intermediate, particularly elementary

Language skills Recognition of words and expressions in an authentic text. Reading for detail without worrying about understanding *every* detail.

Procedure

1. Collect material with parallel texts in different languages including L1 and L2, eg. leaflets, brochures, instruction sheets for cameras, toys, electrical apparatus, etc.

2. Work in pairs. Underline certain words and expressions in the L1 text.

3. Try to find the corresponding words and expressions in the L2 text.

4. Make a list of words and expressions worth learning.

Comments This is an activity using authentic — even difficult — texts in learning to discover and identify specific words or expressions. At elementary level using material to show students they can *use* material even if they don't understand everything. This is a great motivator — students see they can really do something even with their limited knowledge.

Activities

36. Reflecting on a text

Time : 10-15 minutes   **Level :** Intermediate, Advanced

Language skills   Reading comprehension. Discussion of reactions to the content of a text.

Procedure

1. The teacher distributes an L2 text.

2. Discuss first in L1 any expectations or associations the students gain from the title or illustrations to the text.

3. Each student then reads silently through the text and makes notes on his/her reactions and thoughts concerning the content of the text. For example:

    — **What have I learned from the text?**
    — **Do I agree or not?**
    — **What objections can be raised?**
    — **Any personal experiences that are relevant?**
    — **Does it confirm or change my own opinion?**
    — **What else should be taken up in this context?**

4. Work in pairs. Compare notes and discuss different reactions and thoughts on the text.

Comments   An alternative to the conventional reading comprehension exercise in which students answer questions on the text. In reality it is rare that we ask ourselves comprehension questions *after* reading something. Apart from the intentions or expectations we have before reading a text, thoughts and reactions occur *during* the actual reading. This activity serves to make text reading in L2 more natural.

37. Text substitutions

Time : about 20 minutes   **Level :** Intermediate

Language skills Searching the memory for vocabulary; extension of vocabulary. Identifying groups of words which are structurally or semantically similar. Practice of associated structural changes in the text.

Procedure

1. The teacher presents a text in which certain words or phrases have been underlined.

2. Together with the teacher the whole class now makes up L1-substitutions for the underlinings in the text. The teacher writes the substitutions on the board and the students copy in the margin of their text, eg.:

Text in L2	**Substitutions in L1**
"Am <u>Samstag</u> ist <u>Heinz</u> nach Stuttgart gefahren um seine <u>Schwester</u> zu besuchen..."	Monday, Wednesday, the weekend Ulrike, our neighbours, I brother, parents, friend

3. Work in pairs, taking turns to read the text and substituting each underlined word with translations of one of the alternatives in the margin. Continue until all the substitutions have been used.

Comments This activity is well-suited for practising structural changes resulting from the introduction of new elements (eg. possessive adjectives, singular or plural forms, verb tenses, etc.)

Variation Change a text, substituting information about oneself, eg:

> George is a tall, dark-haired man in his early 30's. He is a car salesman and likes good food and playing rugby...

Can be changed to:

I am a . . . in my (teens, 20's. . .)
I am a (student, telephonist. . .) and I like . . .

38. Fill the gaps

Time : about 15 minutes   **Level :** All

Language skills Copying and reading. Vocabulary revision. Guessing from context clues.

Procedure

1. Each student writes a copy of a previously-studied text occasionally omitting words or expressions of particular importance or difficulty, eg:

> Gracias por unos. . . muy interesantes en Madrid.
> ¿ Ahora. . . en Bilbao?

2. Form groups. Pass the text around in each group. Each student reads the text received, mentally filling in the gaps, checking if necessary with the original text.

3. Continue to circulate the texts within the group. Exchange papers afterwards with another group.

Comments May be used to practise writing, spelling with accuracy, and to increase reading speed.

Variations Instead of 1. above, the teacher omits every 8th word from the text and asks students to read, filling-in the gaps (in other words make a cloze-test from the text).

39. Cut and Combine

Time : 10-20 minutes   **Level :** Intermediate to advanced

Language skills Reading and listening comprehension; reading aloud; listening for relevant information to combine text with picture or heading.

Procedure

1. The teacher collects authentic materials such as newspaper cuttings, then does one of the following:

    — separates the article/text from the heading
    — separates the article from the picture
    — cuts the article into two (or more) parts

2. Distribute the cuttings to the students and let them read through what they have received.

3. One student at a time then reads out his or her heading, holds up/ describes the picture or reads out his or her article and waits until someone reads out or produces the corresponding part.

Comments A good active listening activity. Trains the ability to comprehend the general content of a text — or to perceive relevant details which link it with a picture or a heading. A stimulating way of working with authentic materials such as newspaper cuttings.

40. Hard texts - easy tasks

Time : 15-20 minutes   **Level :** Elementary or Intermediate

Language skills *General* comprehension of an authentic text (it must be stressed that it is *general* comprehension, not detailed knowledge).

Procedure

1. Use authentic material such as newspaper or magazine articles.

2. Students work in pairs. They read the text, trying to find out, for example:
    — the main points of the text
    — the general theme of the text
    — answers to simple, general questions that the teacher has prepared.

3. Compare results of pair work in the whole class or by rotating in pairs.

Comments This activity shows that it is not only the language of a text which makes it difficult for students. The degree of difficulty depends on the task set. Can be a rewarding activity for students to work occasionally with authentic material and actually understand some of it, so they can *use* it, even without understanding it all. Be very careful not to kill this interest by demanding too much at lower levels.

Variation Choose authentic material which is not 'solid' text — eg. an advert, menu, programme, sign. Ask only a few, particular questions which students can answer by identifying individual words etc.

41. Answer an advertisement

Time : 30-40 minutes   **Level :** Intermediate, Advanced

Language skills Understanding the language used in classified ads; abbreviations. Language functions of inquiring, giving information, opening and ending a telephone conversation.

Procedure

1. The teacher collects a number of different adverts from a newspaper in L2 (eg. job vacancies, articles for sale, personal column, accommodation wanted).

2. Divide into pairs and distribute the adverts amongst the pairs.

3. Each pair works on its advert, first making sure that they understand it. They then prepare a telephone conversation between the advertiser and the reader. Make notes of words and phrases needed for the conversation.

4. Practise the conversation in pairs, using the advertisement and notes as aids.

5. Act out the conversation in the whole class or by rotating in pairs (see Page 17).

Comments An activity using authentic material to stimulate the students' imagination and creative abilities. Could be followed up by starting a classroom noticeboard for the students to put up notices/advertisements of their own in L2 (objects for sale, wanted, to swap, lost, etc).

Activities

42. Up or down?

Time : 2-5 minutes   **Level :** Elementary

Language skills Recognition of rising and falling intonation in continuous speech.

Procedure

1. Play a recording in L2. Students indicate whether the speaker's voice goes up or down:

2. Play the same — or another — recording. Learners follow the text and mark rising and falling intonation by means of arrows:

3. Discuss why the voice goes up or down in the examples.

Comments This activity recognises the value of teaching intonation receptively first, before asking students to produce intonation patterns. Practise the same sentence, giving it different intonation. Discuss how this affects communication, and what responses might be expected. Suitable for early stages of language learning.

Variation Instead of listening to a whole text recording, it could be divided up by letting students first indicate by means of gestures at each pause, then mark intonation on their texts.

43. Count the questions

Time : 5-10 minutes   **Level :** Elementary, Intermediate

Language skills Recognition and practice of intonation denoting questions in L2.

Procedure

1. Play a recording in L2.

2. Students listen for and note down the number of questions that occur in the recorded material.

3. Compare results, in pairs, then in whole class.

4. Choral repetition in whole class.

Comments An easy introduction to intonation-type activities. Students should note questions, language which *functions* as a question and not only normal question forms. This means all these are "questions".

> *Have you been there?*
> *Really?*
> *You went there by Concorde?*
> *On Tuesday?*

At intermediate level, using a recording containing functional questions can encourage a discussion which makes students more aware of the flexible way language is used. Many native speakers, for example, looking for Grange Road, do not use *Excuse me, could you tell me the way to Grange Road, please,* but ask the much simpler *Excuse me, Grange Road?* It helps to make students aware of this, for both receptive and productive use.

44. Spot the mistakes

Time : 5-10 minutes   **Level :** Elementary, Intermediate

Language skills Aural comprehension. Correction of 'false information'. Practice in the functions of interrupting and correcting.

Procedure

1. The teacher reads aloud a **known** (ie. previously-studied) text to the class but makes an occasional deliberate mistake: eg. "Alan went into the *kitchen* and..." *("garage"* in the text)

2. The class interrupts to correct each mistake without looking at the text.

Comments Ways of interrupting or negating a statement *(No, he didn't/No, they weren't,* etc.) should be revised or presented before commencing the activity. This activity encourages listening which requires a real response (interruption, correction) instead of traditional "comprehension questions".

45. Identify attitudes

Time : 10-15 minutes   **Level :** All

Language skills Active listening for specific features of speech showing particular attitudes.

Procedure

1. The teacher plays a recording in L2 and asks the students to note how many people are involved in the conversation. Check in whole class.

2. Teacher then presents a chart, showing the people involved together with a list of possible attitudes expressed in the conversation, for example:

People	Attitudes				
	Happy	Angry	Uncertain	Impatient	Bored
Man					
Woman					
Boy					

3. The class listens again to the recording and tries to identify the attitudes of each speaker, as indicated by their intonation or tone of voice. Students mark their charts during, or immediately after, listening.

4. Follow up by comparing notes in pairs or small groups and then in whole class.

Comments Active, *detailed* listening for features of the spoken language is important. It helps make students aware of how meaning is conveyed in speech by much more than "words" and "grammar". It is very important for teachers to recognize that such speech factors are not universal and what indicates irritation in one language may not have that meaning in another. In other words, such features do need to be learned in a foreign language. This activity helps students to be more aware of something they frequently do not even recognize. Can be adapted to different levels. At low levels it is best to use short dialogues with a three point attitude scale such as:
ENTHUSIASTIC NEUTRAL   BORED
ANGRY   NEUTRAL   PLEASED
At intermediate levels the chart above may be suitable. At more advanced levels such attitudes as sarcasm, irony, disbelief may be introduced, and more complex speech factors such as rhythm, pitch, speed, may be considered. Often the follow-up is best done with a two-part question:
How does . . . feel? (answered from the chart)
How do you know? (answered in L1, if necessary)

46. True or false?

Time : 10-15 minutes   **Level :** Elementary, Intermediate

Language skills Listening comprehension for specific information. Making notes.

Procedure

1. The teacher prepares a list of statements on a passage for listening comprehension. The list is copied and distributed to each student. Some of the statements are true, others false, according to the information in the given passage. Example:

Statements	Notes
1. La famille habite à Londres. 2. Ils ont deux enfants. 3. L'appartement est trop grand. 4. Madame S. travaille dans une usine.	

2. The teacher plays the recording or reads the text. During this first reading the students mark off on their lists those statements that are false.

3. During the second hearing each student writes corrections in the "notes" column.

4. Form pairs to check and compare notes.

Comments Many students will find this a more encouraging alternative to conventional listening comprehension questions. When correcting it is often natural to reproduce the same structure as the original, thus providing good written and oral practice of that structure. Practises listening and note-taking skills at the same time (an important study-skill).

47. Active listening

Time : 10-15 minutes   **Level :** All

Language skills Listening comprehension for general or specific points in a continuous passage.

Procedure

1. The teacher prepares a few questions in L1 or L2 on the material to be heard by the class. Questions may be of the following kinds:

    a. Simple comprehension questions (eg. *What did the woman buy? How much did it cost?*)

    b. "Detective" questions, which require deeper understanding — interpreting, drawing conclusions, 'reading between the lines' and looking for answers throughout the whole passage (eg. *Which of the characters do you think is lying? Why do you think he was annoyed?*)

    c. Instead of comprehension questions, active listening can involve listening for specific information such as:
        — numbers, prices, weights, etc.
        — names of people or places
        — time expressions
        — politeness phrases

2. The prepared questions are then given to the class. The material is then read or played to the class. All listen specifically for the answers to the questions.

3. Allow time for the students to compare their answers in pairs or small groups before checking in the whole class. The answers may be given in L1 or L2 depending on the level of ability and on the degree of difficulty of the material or of the questions given.

Comments Listening comprehension can be made more active and effective by having something specific to listen for. Even a difficult or authentic piece of recorded material such as a news summary or a genuine conversation can be attempted at lower levels if the question tasks are adapted to the students' ability level. Thus it is *not* the aim to *reproduce* the listening material, but simply to *understand* enough to be able to answer the questions. A good activity for promoting language acquisition.

48. Listening in

Time : about 20 minutes   **Level :** Intermediate, Advanced

Language skills Discussion, active listening for detail, listening for content, correction of particular language mistakes. At higher levels, appropriacy and collocation.

Procedure

1. Record a short teacher-led whole-class discussion. The recording should not be longer than a few (5?) minutes. It is best to use a topic of current interest. A group of a dozen or fewer students is best.

2. Exchange the recordings made by two classes or groups. Play back the unknown recording to the new group.

3. First ask the new group to *summarise* the recording, very briefly.

4. Re-wind the recording and re-play it. This time ask students to signal — by, for example, raising a hand, each time they hear something which they think is a language mistake, or which can be said better in a different way. The teacher should not correct mistakes on the tape at this time, but should discuss only those comments raised by the students.

Comments This shows students clearly that they are listening for two *different* reasons, first for content and then for the details of the language used. New ideas include concentrating on the mistakes which the *students* identify, rather than those which the teacher wishes to take up; treating the correction of mistakes as an important part of the lesson, but in a light-hearted way.

49. Song lyrics

Time : 20-30 minutes **Level :** Post-beginners, Intermediate

Language skills Intensive listening to words not clearly spoken, as they are on most language teaching tapes. Analysing the content of the song lyrics.

Procedure

1. Play a recording of a song in L2.

2. Play again and use the pause button of the recorder to stop after each line. The class tries to make out the words, repeating them for the teacher to write on the board.

3. The students copy the lyrics from the board.

4. Discuss the song lyrics — language, and content; even the 'sounds' such as rhymes, rhythms, alliterations and the associations they give rise to.

5. Sing the song together with the aid of the recording and the written text.

Comments Usually a popular activity with school classes. Students could be encouraged to bring in recordings of their own. Sometimes the lyrics are written on the cover of LP records.

50. What is it?

Time : 10-15 minutes   **Level :** All

Language skills Descriptive adjectives of shape, feel, texture, weight, size, etc. Generalising expressions *(sort of, kind of, it feels like...it's made of).* Question forms.

Procedure
1. One volunteer comes to the front, stands facing the class, hands behind back.

2. Teacher places an object (for example, a potato, a cotton reel, a paper clip) into the volunteer's hand. The object should not be seen by either the volunteer or the rest of the class.

3. The volunteer tries to describe the object (shape, size, texture, material, etc.) after which the class guess what it is, or ask questions to get further information.

4. The volunteer then shows the object, when someone has guessed correctly.

5. Repeat with a new object and a new volunteer.

Comments The game de-focuses, and allows real communication to develop. May also be done in small groups. Although this is a "game" the language required may be quite demanding. In choosing objects and students for this activity remember it is being used for language teaching — it is the language which is important! Some language preparation may be necessary.

51. Guess the object

Time : 10-20 minutes   **Level :** All, mainly intermediate

Language skills Question forms. Vocabulary revision or extension.

Procedure

1. Divide into groups. Each group decides on an object, for which they know the word in L2.

2. The others then try to guess the object by asking questions requiring a *Yes/No* answer.

3. A limit of, say, 10 or 20 questions may be set. Examples of types of question:

> **Is it made of wood?**
> **Can you eat it?**
> **Is it expensive?**
> **Is it bigger than an apple?**
> **Can you find it in the home?**
> **Is there one in this room?**
> **Have I got one?**

Comments May be adapted to suit different levels — question-types can be prepared first; the objects could be selected from words encountered in previous lessons, and so on.

52. Mime interpretations

Time : about 20 minutes   **Level :** Elementary, Intermediate

Language skills Use of gestures. Relating words and meaning to non-verbal communication.

Procedure

1. Work in pairs. Each pair prepares a short "silent conversation" using only mime gestures.

2. Form groups of 4 (2 pairs). One pair in each group performs their scene, while the other pair observes and tries to interpret the scene.

3. The observing pair then re-enacts the scene, this time with words (in L2) they think appropriate. The first pair comments (in L1) afterwards on the interpretation.

4. Change roles, the observing pair now performs their "silent conversation".

"Yes, I think I've got it . . . You want two stalls . . . Saturday . . . Matinée . . . 24th August."

Comments While focussing attention on non-verbal exchanges, this activity also generates much verbal activity, at both points 1 and 3 above.

53. Seek advice

Time : 15-30 minutes   **Level :** Intermediate, Advanced

Language skills Describing a problem, asking questions, offering advice. Active listening and summarising.

Procedure

1. Work in small groups. One person in each group *briefly* outlines a *problem*. The problem may be real or imagined; it is best if it is as concrete as possible:

    My girlfriend has left me for someone else.

    I find it impossible to study at home.

    I can never make up my mind about anything.

2. One of the others in the group now acts as *counsellor* and tries to help the first person to solve the problem. The others in the group listen and act as *observers*. The counsellor should ask questions such as *Why was that? How do you know? What do you mean by that? Would you explain that a little more?* etc.

3. When the conversation is over, the observers give comments.

4. Follow up in the whole class. The observers from each group summarise what happened.

Comments Steps 3 and 4 could be conducted in L1 or L2, depending on the level of ability. If encouraged, this activity could lead to a fruitful discussion of real problems experienced by the class as a whole or by individuals in the class. Most suited to more advanced levels. By working with real problems instead of fictitious text-book problems, the activity focuses on solutions rather than the language used.

54. Double discussion

Time : 20-30 minutes   **Level :** Intermediate

Language skills Topic-related vocabulary and phrases. Giving opinions, arguing for and against, agreeing and disagreeing.

Procedure

1. Agree on a topic for discussion in the class.

2. In small groups, discuss the topic first in L1. Each student notes down key words and phrases which may have to be checked in a dictionary.

3. Look up words and phrases. Make notes of L2 versions.

4. Form new groups and discuss the topic again, this time in L2, with the help of notes.

Comments This activity prepares students for discussing in the foreign language by collecting ideas quickly and easily in stages 1-2 so that they may concentrate on *how* to express the ideas in stage 4. Too often discussions in L2 fail because students are searching simultaneously for *what* to say, and *how* to say it.

55. Guided role play

Time : 20-40 minutes | **Level :** Particularly Intermediate, Advanced

Language skills Functional phrases appropriate to particular situations, stress patterns, general functions, eg. asking for information, apologising, showing surprise, interrupting, etc.

Procedure

1. The teacher suggests, or students choose, a conversational situation involving two people. The teacher suggests a series of questions to help students to build a guide to the situation. Example questions could be:

   Who are the people?
   What are they talking about?
   Are they pleased or annoyed? etc.

   It is best at more advanced levels if the situation involves some sort of mis-understanding or disagreement.

2. Each pair constructs a guide for the role play in their *own* language, L1. The guide is constructed using "Say that. . .", "Ask if. . ." etc. This encourages students to use a variety of language in L2, rather than encouraging literal translation. Here is an example guide:

Situation. B promised to lend **A** a tennis racket yesterday. **A** plans to use the racket to play a game this evening.

A	B
Ask if B has remembered the racket.	
	Say you have forgotten. Apologise and say you didn't forget deliberately.
Show you are annoyed. Explain that you need the racket to play this evening.	
	Explain why you forgot.
Say you won't ask B again!	
	Say you think A is being unreasonable.
Agree. Apologise.	
	Suggest A asks someone else who might be able to help.

Further examples of useful practices which involve some element of "disagreement" are: buying a sweater with a friend who disagrees, explaining you have lost something you have borrowed, apologising for breaking something/upsetting a cup of tea, etc.

3. Practise the role play in pairs using the prepared guide. Sometimes it is a good idea to do it twice, with the students taking the roles the other way round the second time. Students should only look at one half of the guide and cover the other half while they are doing the role play.

4. One or more pairs can take turns to "perform" for the class.

5. The language students use, and the language they need to perform general functions — such as showing annoyance, or apologising, can be discussed after each "performance".

Comments The first time students attempt the guided role play the teacher may need to give some help with language after the guide is prepared, but before students perform. Later, it is better to give students as much opportunity as possible to prepare in their own way and for the teacher to use the comments on the students' performances as the best time to present the language students need.

Variation At lower levels it is possible to ask students to produce more situational dialogues — ordering in a restaurant, buying train tickets, at the lost property office etc.

56. Improvised role play

Time : 20-30 minutes   **Level :** Intermediate to Advanced

Language skills Free interaction and improvisation within an agreed framework (situation and roles).

Procedure

1. Agree in the whole class on a situation for a role play, for example:

    — **In the home: An unexpected letter arrives.**
    — **At a restaurant: Sharing a table with strangers.**
    — **At the disco: An unpleasant incident.**

2. Discuss the situation together in more detail. Invite suggestions from the class. Questions to ask could be:

    — **How many people are involved? Who are they?**
    — **What are their relationships? Are they happy/friendly/ angry?**
    — **What *has* happened? What *is* happening? What's *going* to happen?**
    — **What sort of things are they saying to each other?**

3. Divide the class into groups, each group with the number required to play the roles agreed on in 2. above.

4. Give students time to prepare their own roles quietly in more detail (character, likes/dislikes, attitude to situation, etc.) The role plays are then improvised in the groups, working simultaneously.

5. Follow up with a short oral report from each group on how the improvisation developed.

Comments In a class which is unfamiliar with role plays it is advisable to prepare points 1. and 2. thoroughly before starting the group work. Further assistance can be given by collecting useful words or phrases in the whole class as a preliminary to the improvisation.

Variation Use a text as a starting-point for improvised role plays. The students assume the roles of people in the text and build on the information given.

57. Discuss and report

Time : 20-40 minutes   **Level :** Intermediate, Advanced

Language skills Listening, making notes and reporting from the notes.

Procedure

1. Decide in the whole class on a topic for discussion.

2. Divide into small groups and discuss the topic for a given length of time. Each student makes notes on the main points discussed. Make a group summary of the discusssion at the end of the planned time.

3. At a pre-arranged time, cross-reporting groups are formed (see page 17). Each student in turn then reports to the new group what was discussed in his/her original group.

Comments This activity places a responsibility on each individual student ·to follow a group discussion and to report what was said. This skill needs a lot of practice if it is to be done well.

Variations 1. The discussions may be based on previously studied material.
2. Each group discusses a different aspect of the same topic.
3. Each group chooses its own topic for discussion, from a given list or completely freely.

58. Work visits

Time : about 30 minutes   **Level :** Intermediate, Advanced

Language skills Vocabulary connected with different jobs. Question and answer techniques. The language of eliciting and expanding/avoiding answers.

"I did ask you not to touch anything."

Procedure

1. Form pairs. Each pair chooses a "work place" to "visit". One student in each pair prepares to act as host, and talk about the work; the other prepares questions for the role of visitor.

    School students, who have little or no experience of work, will need considerable help with the kind of questions they can ask. Examples could include:

    > **What time do you start work?**
    > **How long have you worked here?**
    > **How much holiday do you usually get?**
    > **Are you well paid?**
    > **What is the best/worst thing about your job?**
    > **How do you spend your day?**
    > **Do you have a lot of contact with other people?**
    > **Do you make your own decisions?**
    > **What is the most interesting/boring part of your job?**
    > **What sort of machinery or equipment do you use?**

Activities

With older students, particularly adults who are working and can obviously talk about the particular job they do, concentrate on the work place.

2. Carry out the "study visit" in pairs, one student asking the questions and the second giving the information,

3. When all the pairs are ready, act one or more of the study visits in the whole class.

Comments This activity works best with adults or older teenagers who are thinking about the kind of work they may do. It gives students an opportunity to talk about their own jobs and work interests. Children could perhaps talk about a parent's job.

59. Debate

Time : 45-60 minutes   **Level :** Mostly Advanced

Language skills Stating views on a given topic, agreeing and disagreeing, asking questions, summarising.

Procedure

1. Agree in the whole class on a topic for debate. A topic of current interest is often best.

2. Distribute the following roles amongst the students:
    — **Chairpersons:** two people to lead the debate, put questions, interrupt, summarise views expressed and keep a check on the time.
    — **Panel:** 3-5 well-known 'personalities', prepared to give their own views and 'start the ball rolling'.
    — **Audience:** the rest of the class, consisting of various experts, representatives of different authorities, organisations, interest groups, political parties and members of the public.

3. All now prepare their roles, individually or, where appropriate, in groups. Write notes of what to say — viewpoints, questions, useful words or phrases.

4. Establish a set time for the debate, say 20-30 minutes. Hold the debate.

5. Follow up by talking about how it worked out. Discuss and follow up important language errors.

Comments A good way to start the debate is to first study a topical event, perhaps through press cuttings or a TV programme. In this way all students have a chance to 'warm up' to the subject and relevant vocabulary can be introduced.

Variation If possible you could record or even video the debate to make it more like a TV recording. If this is done, use the recording in the follow-up (step 5 above).

60. Own dialogues

Time : 10-20 minutes   **Level :** Elementary, Intermediate

Language skills Intensive practice of dialogue through choral repetition and pairwork; translation of natural spoken language.

Procedure

1. Together, in the whole class, make up a short, simple conversation — in L1 — between two people, using language you would like to learn in L2.

2. The teacher writes the dialogue in L1 on the board, and an L2 translation beside the original.

3. The teacher reads the L2 dialogue phrase-by-phrase and the students repeat in chorus. Do this a few times.

4. Practise the dialogue in pairs, changing roles.

5. The students copy the L2 dialogue from the board.

6. The teacher rubs out the L2 dialogue from the board.

7. Pairs take turns to repeat the dialogue aided by the L1-version on the board and, if necessary, by their own notes.

Comments The preparatory work of constructing a dialogue, rather than using a ready-made one, generally increases motivation and interest. Suitable from beginners' level.

61. Construct-a-dialogue

Time : 5-15 minutes   **Level :** Intermediate, Advanced

Language skills Recall of vocabulary and structures around a chosen theme or situation. At higher levels, appropriate, as well as accurate, choice of language.

Procedure

1. Decide in the whole class on a topic or situation for a dialogue.

2. Form pairs. One in each pair, working alone, writes an opening line on a piece of paper and then passes the paper to his partner.

3. The other then writes a reply and passes the paper back.

4. Continue until the dialogue seems ready.

5. Practise the dialogue together in pairs.

6. Finally, the dialogues can be performed by the pairs in turn for the rest of the class.

Comments Considerable scope for flexibility and creativity, particularly at more advanced levels. This also resembles real life in that the responses are created spontaneously. A good example of an extension exercise at lower and intermediate levels. Notice that students' dialogues are produced, practised, and performed without the teacher "correcting" or "improving" them (unless students *ask* for help during stages 2-4). This approach, where the *whole* (the dialogue, and ability to communicate in a complete situation) is the focus of activity, not the *part* (word, phrase, line of dialogue, or "mistake") is strange for some teachers. We do not suggest such activities all the time, but they are an important part of a balanced language learning programme. Too much attention to parts and mistakes, with no opportunity to feel the success, or partial success, of managing the whole, is de-motivating and makes the task of learning a foreign language unrewarding and even impossible. Teachers will need to explain to students that activities like these are different from normal textbook exercises which place great emphasis on accuracy of details. Students will find this new style of practice rewarding if they understand *why* they are doing them.

62. Opinions and objections

Time : 15-30 minutes **Level :** Intermediate, Advanced

Language skills Intensive practice of the functions of expressing opinions and making objections.

Procedure

1. Each student, individually or in small groups, thinks up a statement in L1 — as provocative as possible — beginning *I/we think that...; I/We don't think...; In my/our opinion...* etc. Examples:

    > **I think that people should retire at 50.**
    > **I don't think women should play football.**
    > **In my opinion schools are a waste of time and money.**

2. Each person or group in turn says their statement, and they are translated into L2 and written up on the board. About 8 statements should be enough for the activity.

3. Everyone works alone, thinking up objections or counter-arguments to some or all of the statements on the board. Use dictionaries if necessary.

4. Form small groups. Compare objections and counter-arguments.

5. Go through the statements, one by one, in the whole class, each group suggesting their counter-arguments.

Comments The final stage could, at more advanced levels, expand into spontaneous class discussions. Alternatively, the activity could be concluded by working in pairs and going once more through the statements and — with or without visual support — making counter-arguments.

63. Hooks

Time : 20-30 minutes   **Level :** All

Language skills Free association to extend vocabulary. Explaining reasons for associations.

Procedure

1. The teacher gives the class a word, which each student writes in the middle of a blank piece of paper. Students then draw a circle around the word, and ten hooks off the circle; for example:

2. Students have, say, 5 minutes working individually to write on the end of each hook one word they associate with the central word.

3. In groups of three the students then compare what they have 'hooked'. The first student reads out his/her words. The others underline on their own papers any words they have in common and write in new words. The second and third students read their own words in the same way.

4. Each group counts the number of different words they have produced (maximum 30).

5. Follow up in the whole class. Individual students can explain words new to the other students. More advanced classes can explain why they made particular associations and discuss them.

Comments Students are likely to discover that they have very different associations for the given word. More advanced classes are likely to score higher in point 4 above.
Because people are more *personally* involved, both in their own associations and the more surprising ones produced by other students, they are more likely to learn new words introduced by other members of the class.

Further examples of starting words:

Home	**Red**	**School**
Warm	**Language**	**America**
Night	**Dream**	**Excited**

64. Rhyme time

Time : 20-30 minutes   **Level :** Intermediate, Advanced

Language skills Pronunciation. Rhyming sounds. Vocabulary searching. Association of ideas and creative language skills.

Procedure

1. Agree on a topic in the class (eg. City life, love, people, leisure, etc.) to write a poem or song lyric about. Write the topic on the board.

2. Make a list of words in L2 that the students associate with the topic. Do this in the whole class and write the words on the board. Then try to find words to rhyme with these words. For example:

   > city - pretty
   > cars - bazaars
   > street - meet, neat, feet, treat

3. In pairs or small groups — write short poems/song texts with the help of the rhyming words. (The poems may be only a few lines.)

4. Read the poems to each other or to the class.

Comments Enjoyment is usually increased by making this a pair or group activity. A great deal is lost if, for example, stage 3 is done as an individual activity, when it can easily become a matter of competition and prestige.

65. Tell a joke

Time : 20-30 minutes **Level :** All

Language skills Use of informal, vivid narrative style. Short, light-hearted translations. Reading aloud and "timing", ie, speaking to create a particular effect.

Procedure

1. In pairs — tell each other a joke in L1.

2. By working together, translate both jokes into L2 and write down the translations. Use a dictionary if necessary, or ask the teacher for help.

3. When all pairs are ready, come together and take it in turns to read out the jokes.

Comments If students find it difficult to think up a joke, have a few in reserve that have been cut out of newspapers or magazines to be adapted and translated into L2. It is advisable to begin with very short jokes perhaps only one or two lines, or even riddles, to encourage full participation. Be careful of any joke depending on a pun — they are often impossible to translate. Using jokes prepared by other students means they are usually at the right linguistic level for the others. Even those who have never before told a joke in their lives can gain confidence this way.

Variation Make a classroom "joke board", where the best jokes are written out carefully and pinned to the board. Hang the board outside the class-room so other students can read it.

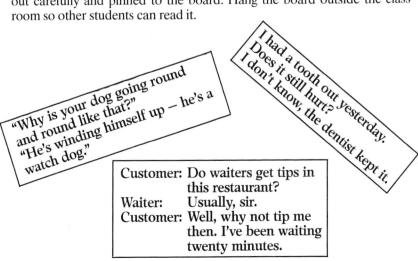

"Why is your dog going round and round like that?"
"He's winding himself up – he's a watch dog."

I had a tooth out yesterday.
Does it still hurt?
I don't know, the dentist kept it.

Customer: Do waiters get tips in this restaurant?
Waiter: Usually, sir.
Customer: Well, why not tip me then. I've been waiting twenty minutes.

Activities

66. Continue the story

Time : 20-30 minutes   **Level :** Intermediate, Advanced

Language skills Extension of vocabulary and structures previously introduced in a text or recording. Verb forms, especially past tenses. Connecting words. Creative thinking and writing in L2.

Procedure

1. A story is chosen by the class or the teacher. The story can be a text, a recording or a series of pictures.

2. Work in pairs. Each pair extends the story in any way they wish and writes down their version, using a dictionary if necessary.

3. Different pairs read their version aloud for the whole class, or by rotating in pairs (see page 17)

Comments Much language teaching, particularly at lower levels, concentrates on structural accuracy or on 'useful' language for communication. Many students enjoy this form of activity which instead stimulates the imagination and encourages *creative* use of the foreign language.

67. Associations

Time : 20-40 minutes   **Level :** Intermediate, Advanced

Language skills Vocabulary associations; creative writing.

Procedure

1. Choose a word or a topic in the class, eg. "Summer", "Water", "Happiness".

2. Students associate freely to the word chosen and take turns to call out their associations. The teacher writes on the board the words called out.

3. Form small groups. Each group chooses 10-15 words from the list on the board and makes up a short story or poem around those words.

4. Each group in turn tells its story or recites its poem to the whole class.

Comments The opportunity of associating to a word or theme can produce a surprising variety of ideas if allowed to develop freely. Spontaneity should be encouraged, but unusual connections with the theme should be challenged so that the student concerned explains the association.

Variation An alternative way to begin is for the teacher to say a word. Any student then says a word he/she associates with the previous word and so on. Continue around the class, each time associating only with the last word spoken. This should be done at a brisk pace. The difference is that this technique often produces a *sequence* of ideas — ie, the outline of a 'story'.

68. Letters to the editor

Time : 40-60 minutes   **Level :** Intermediate, Advanced

Language skills Letter writing. Expression of opinions. Turning spoken ideas into language appropriate to a letter. Aural comprehension of letters read out by other groups.

Procedure

1. Work in small groups to compose a letter in L2 to a magazine. Use a dictionary if needed. The letter may be about something of general concern, some problem or something one wants to change or complain about.

2. Each group reads out its letter to the class.

3. Each group chooses, from among the letters read out, the one it wants to answer and then works out a reply. More than one group can choose to reply to the same letter.

4. When all groups are ready, the replies can be read out, group by group.

5. Afterwards the various letters and the suggested replies can be discussed in small groups, and followed up in the whole class or by cross reporting (see page 17).

Comments Provides much scope for discussing, arguing, stating opinions in small groups, at more advanced levels of language learning. Some sample letters from a magazine may help to generate ideas prior to group work.

69. Shouting and whispering

Time : 3-5 minutes   **Level :** All, especially elementary

Language skills Pronunciation, stress, intonation.

Procedure

1. Choral repetition after teacher/tape model. Normal voice quality and volume.

2. Students are asked to imagine that the teacher is somewhat deaf and they have to shout their choral responses.

3. The students are then asked to imagine that this has led to complaints from the neighbours. They should therefore now whisper their responses as softly as possible.

4. Revert to normal voice and volume for final repetition.

Comments This activity takes the focus away from the language learning. The students concentrate on shouting and whispering instead of on repeating "correctly". This actually helps students' performance.

Activities

70. The witness

Time : 10-15 minutes   **Level :** All

Language skills Describing people (features, clothes, age, build etc.). Asking questions about personal descriptions *(How tall is he? What was his hair like?* etc.) Checking and eliciting extra information.

"Men—you're all the same!"

Procedure

1. The teacher has a picture of a person. Say that a crime has been committed and that you have a picture of the suspect.

2. Divide the class into pairs. One in each pair is *the witness* and the other *a policeman.*

3. Show the picture for *5 seconds* to the witnesses only. The policemen must look away.

4. The witness in each pair then tries to describe the person in the picture in as much detail as possible to his/her partner. The policeman listens and asks questions to improve the description.

5. Finally, let the policemen see the picture. Discuss mistakes and any misunderstandings (of content, not language).

Comments A role-play activity that makes the pair work both challenging and meaningful as 'real' communication. May also be used to describe an object. The activity may give rise to a discussion on the difficulty of describing from memory someone or something only briefly seen and on the reliability of the evidence.

71. Pictures from memory

Time : 15-30 minutes   **Level :** All

Language skills Descriptive past tense. Prepositions of place. Phrases to describe positions on a picture *(at the bottom/top, in the background* etc.) Making notes in L2 and then describing from notes.

Procedure

1. Ask everyone to bring a picture from a newspaper or magazine to the next lesson. The picture should be quite detailed.

2. Divide the class into small groups. One person in each group begins by holding up his/her picture for 5 seconds. The others then make notes in L2 of as many details as they can remember.

3. Everyone then takes in turn to read from his/her notes, after which the picture is shown again and differences between notes and picture checked.

4. When a group has finished, swap pictures with another group and repeat the procedure.

Comments The amount of guidance needed will depend on the level of the group and the choice of pictures.

Variation Bring *news pictures* from the previous week. Students try to remember — or guess — what news item the picture illustrates. Go from L1 to L2 or, if possible, directly into L2.

72. Information gaps

Time : 15-30 minutes　　　　　　　　**Level :** Any

Language skills Asking for and giving specific information, the functions of agreeing, disagreeing, interrupting, etc. that are appropriate to the particular situation.

What is an "information gap"? We do not speak without a reason. The reason is usually because one person has a piece of information or opinion which the other person does not know. The purpose of speaking is to pass the information, opinion etc. across the "information gap". Any activity involving two students each having their own set of information which is not known to the other student, contains the essentials of an information gap activity.

Why is the information gap important? A lot of traditional language teaching involved students doing exercises for no particular reason — they were not communicating anything, they were simply doing formal practice. Most good modern language teaching is based on a recognition of the fact that *communication* is an *essential* element in the use of language. Information gap activites ensure the classroom activities involve some element of communication. They may vary from very formal — the simple exchange of information — to more complex exchanges which involve not only information, but ideas and attitudes. They are important because they are a step away from formal practice towards an activity which more closely mirrors the use of language outside the classroom.

Different kinds of information gap activity.

1. The "gap" may be created by the teacher (or textbook writer) by, for example, giving each student in a pair a card containing information. The activity consists of students exchanging certain information with each other. (See Example 1)

2. Each student completes a questionnaire according to his or her own experience or opinion. Students then check whether their partners have done the same things, share the same opinions etc. (See Example 2)

3. The information gap is based on some sort of puzzle where each of the partners has *some* of the information needed for its solution. In this case a small additional variation is possible where the two sets of information together are still not quite sufficient for the students to complete the activity and one or other of the students must contribute something as a result of privately known information, logical deduction etc. (See Examples 3, 4)

4. Each student is given a short description of one half of a situation. The activity then consists of building the conversation appropriate to the situation. (See Example 5)

Procedure

1. Divide the class into pairs.

2. Give each student the appropriate "half" of an information gap activity. Explain that they must not look at each other's information. It is a good idea if the information given to the students includes the instructions for what they are required to do. It is often helpful for one student's information to contain the information *You start,* while the other student's includes *Your partner will start.*

3. Students prepare for a few moments silently.

4. Students do the activity, without further preparation by the teacher.

5. One or more pairs "performs" for the class. If all pairs are working on the same activity, after each "performance" other students are invited to comment, and both the teacher and students make comments on how the language can be improved.

Comments Even at the lowest levels it is possible to use information gap activities based on simple information (price lists, diaries, list of TV programmes with times and titles, timetables, lists of theatres with addresses and name of plays, etc.) It is also possible to use the kind of "fill-in" activities where students contribute from their own experience. At more advanced levels students may be invited to prepare opinions (rather than facts), and to build quite complex situational dialogues.

Variations 1. The teacher may choose to prepare the class by giving them some of the useful vocabulary and phrases they may need.

2. Particularly at more advanced levels, situational-type activities can be made more interesting if the information given to the two students does not exactly agree so that they cannot predict the whole conversation in advance. The situation should involve some mis-match of information, so that disagreement or misunderstanding is possible.

3. As an alternative to presenting the two students with information in print (on cards etc.) one, or even both students may be presented with information by listening to a short recording.

Example 1

A Fill in the missing names, and the names of the streets. Your partner has some other information.

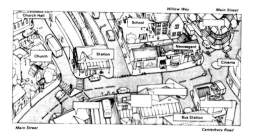

B Fill in the missing names, and the names of the streets. Your partner has some other information.

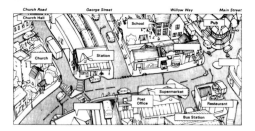

Example 2

Fill in these tables. In the first one, put a ✓ to show what kind of films you *usually like*, or *usually don't like*.

In the second one put a ✓ to show which films you have *seen*, and which ones you *enjoyed*.

Like	don't like			Like	don't like
		Westerns	Space films		
		Historical films	Horror films		
		Cartoons	Musicals		

	Seen	Enjoyed
Any James Bond film		
Any Superman film		
Any 'Star Wars' film		
Any Woody Allen film		

Write down the name of the best film you have seen in the last year:

Example 3

A There are eight buildings in the High Street. Can you identify them all? Your partner has some more information.

The bank is next to the chemist's on the north side of the street. There is a pub between the newsagent's and the bank.

The supermarket is between the butcher's and the post office.

B There are eight buildings in the High Street. Can you identify them all? Your partner has some more information.

The teashop is at the East end of the street opposite the newsagent's. It is next door to the butcher's. The pub is between the newsagent's and the bank, on the opposite side of the road.

Example 4
Both students have the frame

PAIR WORK

A Your partner has the other clues! Fill in the crossword together.

Across
6. Is there _____ in there for me?
8. I've been hurrying so I am out of _____ .
14. I'll do it if I'm _____ to.
15. You do it to a story.

Down
4. You need them on when it is dark.
5. I'll meet you on the _____ .
10. Said yes.
13. Not short.

B Your partner has the other clues! Fill in the crossword together.

Across
3. It tells the time.
7. Young woman
11. A holiday place.
16. Students do it.

Down
1. It lives in the sea.
2. Not less.
9. A kind of animal.
12. Not closed.

Examples 1-4 are all from *Meeting Point*, Michael Lewis, Language Teaching Publications, 1984.

Example 5

You: Work until 5 o'clock every day from Monday to Friday. You live in the centre of town. It is Friday morning.

The situation: You are not doing anything special on Saturday or Sunday. You planned to go to see a film with a friend this evening. Earlier the friend telephoned to say he had a bad cold so he did not want to go to the cinema. You want to see the film so you think you will go on your own. Here are the details of the film from the local paper.

> REGAL. Mon–Sat. Doors Open 2pm
> LCP 7.35 (exc. Sat 8pm)
>
> ## ARTHUR
> From Sun.
> **LAST DAYS OF ROME**

Your partner will start.

You: Want to go to see a film called 'Arthur'. It is on at the Odeon this week (until Sunday). The Odeon is right in the town centre.

The situation: It is Friday morning. You are going away to visit some friends on Saturday and Sunday. You work late on Friday evenings, until 7.30. There is a bus to the town centre just after. It takes 10 minutes. You don't want to go to the cinema on your own. Find out if your partner would like to go. You are not sure when the film starts. Try to make an arrangement (when and where will you meet?) which suits you both.

You start: *Do you fancy going to see 'Arthur'?*

From *Partners 1*, Michael Lewis, Language Teaching Publications, 1982.

73. Own information gaps

Time: 15-30 minutes　　　　　　**Level:** Elementary, Intermediate

Language skills Asking for and giving specific information, such as prices, times, names of products, places, etc.

Procedure

1. The teacher presents a model of a simple information-gap exercise (see previous activity) such as the one below:

Price list at a newsagent's

A		B	
Marlborough	£1-10	Marlborough	_____
After Eight	£1-20	After Eight	_____
The Times	28p	The Times	_____
Dunhill	_____	Dunhill	£1-25
Mars	_____	Mars	22p
The Telegraph	_____	The Telegraph	24p

2. Work in pairs. One in each pair has sheet A, the other sheet B. Ask each other about the missing prices and fill in the answers given. Each student has his own sheet.

3. Check afterwards with your partner that the notes taken were correct.

4. Now ask the students to make their own similar information-gap exercises. Another example is telephone lists:
   — Each pair first makes a list of names.
   — Each person then makes up telephone numbers for half the names on the list. A takes, for example, the top half of the list, while B takes the bottom half.
   — Ask each other, in pairs, for the missing telephone numbers. Fill in on own list.
   — Check afterwards against partner's list.

Comments The same principle can be used to make information gaps with the following:

Menus (with prices)
Diaries (times and dates for activities)
List of names (professions and interests)
TV programmes (times, titles)

Timetables (destinations, times)
Theatre guides (addresses, names of plays)
Restaurants (specialities)

Variations 1. Each student draws a sketch of his/her own house/flat. In pairs take turns to ask each other questions about the layout, number of rooms, size, doors, windows, storeys, etc.

2. Each student draws a sketch of the area where he/she lives. In pairs take turns to ask each other questions about how to get there, neighbours, buildings, etc.

74. Puzzles

Time : 5-30 minutes   **Level :** All

Language skills Reading for specific information, *using* the information for a specific purpose i.e. solving the problem.

What are puzzles? Any kind of problem which has a specific solution is presented in linguistic form. Examples would include logical problems, mathematical problems, psychological games.

Why are puzzles important? We do not use language in a vacuum — it is used for a purpose. Most young people enjoy solving puzzles so that the task they are set is motivating and, instead of reading for the sake of reading, they read for a purpose which is nothing directly to do with language teaching. Instead of *learning* to *use* the language, they *use* the language in order to *learn* it.

The puzzles are presented in L2. From a language point of view the main purpose of the activity is that the students can understand, to the point that they can use, a real natural L2 text. If students wish to solve the problems in L2, this is all to the good, but teachers should not insist. It is still a useful language teaching activity if students speak L1 while solving the problem — the emphasis is on them *understanding* the written material presented to them.

Procedure

1. The students work in pairs or small groups to try to solve the puzzles.

2. If there are difficulties, groups may consult with each other, or with the teacher to see whether people can provide either linguistic help, or help with the puzzle itself.

Comments Puzzles emphasise the use of language for a purpose, and encourage more co-operative attitudes in the classroom. The emphasis is on the *task* and the *process* of solving the task, rather than on the language which is used while they are solving it. In this way language acquisition is promoted.

Often teachers will need to simplify, adapt or translate the puzzles, but the original ideas for puzzles can be found in children's books, logic puzzle magazines, word puzzle books etc. Some examples are given on the next two pages. You may copy the examples to use with your classes.

Two Problems

Can you answer these questions. The obvious answer is always wrong!

1. A clock strikes six in five seconds. How long does it take to strike twelve? (Not 10 seconds).

2. A fast train leaves London for Brighton at the same time as a slow train leaves Brighton for London. The fast train goes at 70mph. The slow train goes at 40mph. It is 50 miles from London to Brighton. Which train is further from London when they meet? You can do this in your head — no pen or paper!

How do you see things?

a. The dark figure is watching the others. He feels alone.

b. The dark figure has just arrived. He is keen to join the party.

c. The dark figure is looking for a particular person in the crowd.

d. The dark figure is worried. He is annoyed at the others enjoying themselves.

a. They are old but happy together.

b. They are old but still live active, interesting lives.

c. They seem to be making a sad, perhaps final, journey.

d. They are lost and looking for somewhere to stay.

Which description is closest to how you see the pictures?

Guilty party

There are only two suspects. The police pick them both up and take them to their new computer centre. The new centre has a 100% reliable lie-detector. Fred, one of the suspects, mumbled something which nobody could hear — except the lie detector.

"There you are — Fred has just confessed his guilt" said the other suspect, Dave.

This message came up on the lie detector's screen. "The guilty man has told only lies; everything the innocent man said was true." Can you work out who was guilty?

Funny football

Two boys like to play football but the only place where they can play is a field near their home. Unfortunately this field is not flat. It slopes quite steeply. After a while they notice that for every two goals scored uphill, three are scored downhill. The game has a strange rule — the winner is the first player to score 18 goals. So that the game is fair, when one of the players has scored nine they change ends.

As usual, the game begins by tossing a coin to decide who will play in which direction first. If you won the toss would you play the first half uphill or downhill, or would it really make no difference?

Who went where?

Five people come from five *different* towns. They went to five different places for their holidays. Can you fill in the table?

Alan is not from York; he, not Sally, went to Rome.
For the girl who went to Greece, Bristol is home.
Anna enjoyed the sun in Spain everyday.
John, from Glasgow, didn't go to the USA.
Mary, from Oxford, didn't take the car.
Who comes from Norwich? Who went to the USSR?

	Comes from	Went to
Alan		
Sally		
Anna		
John		
Mary		

75. Our country

Time : 30-60 minutes   **Level :** Intermediate, Advanced

Language skills Interview techniques. Vocabulary for various aspects of the students' home country, including *explaining* ideas which cannot be directly translated, such as special foods, organizations, etc.

Procedure

1. Divide the class into two halves: *Tourists* and *Guides.* The Tourists imagine they know little or nothing about the home country. The Guides have the job of giving information about the home country.

2. Make a list together in the whole class of topics or areas that could be covered, for example:

   — incomes, taxes, employment
   — food, drink, shopping
   — children, family life, child care
   — schools, education
   — social life, leisure, entertainment
   — tourism, geography, travel
   — customs, traditions, holidays

3. Agree to work on one topic or area of interest at a time. The Tourists work in pairs and discuss what they want to find out, drawing up a number of questions to ask the Guides. The Guides, meanwhile, also working in pairs, prepare the information they are going to give the Tourists about the home country.

4. Form groups of 4 — two Tourists and two Guides. The Guides begin by talking about the topic area chosen and the Tourists put their questions as appropriate during the role play.

5. Follow up in the whole class by summarising important details of information the Tourists "found out" about the home country.

6. Choose another topic area and repeat the activity, this time reversing the roles.

Comments Best for more advanced classes, but can be adapted for lower levels, as a simple role play extension activity following the study of similar information about the country of the target language.

Activities

The ability to talk about their own country in the foreign language is a common need for students when meeting people from other countries. The whole area of "talking about home" is often neglected in language teaching, as students study the culture of the target language. This activity emphasises a useful skill in encouraging students to concentrate on the *language* they need, as the ideas they are talking about are familiar.

In a multi-lingual class, with students from different countries, this activity could be adapted to become a genuine exchange of information about the countries represented.

76. Make conversation

Time : about 45 minutes

Level : mostly adult beginners; smaller classes

Language skills Imitation of sentences spoken in L2. Making written copies of sentences from board. Language analysis of same sentences.

Procedure

1. A small group of students sit around a table with a tape recorder and microphone plus an empty tape, ready for recording. Make sure that each student can operate the recorder. The rest of the class are observers. The teacher stands behind the group or sits at the same table.

2. Anyone begins the conversation by saying something in L1 — whatever feels natural at the time. It is better to keep to short, simple sentences, *Where do you live, Marie? What did you have for breakfast, John? Are you tired, Anne? It's hot, isn't it?*

3. The teacher says the translation of the sentence slowly and clearly, repeating it once or twice.

4. The student who spoke first tries to imitate the L2 sentence with the help of the teacher until it sounds right.

5. That student then starts the tape recorder and says the L2 sentence slowly and clearly into the microphone, then stops the tape with the pause button.

6. Another student in the group answers the question, or says something else in L1.

7. The procedure in 3,4,5 is repeated. When this has also been recorded, the conversation continues in the same way until 10-15 sentences have been recorded on the tape.

8. Re-wind the tape and play back the whole recording. Go back and listen again, this time stopping after each sentence. Check that everyone understands/remembers what was said.

9. Play back the recording a third time, pausing after each sentence. The teacher writes each sentence on the board. Students copy the sentences into their books. The students or teacher may also comment on points of interest.

10. Practise a small number of points arising from the recorded conversation. Make vocabulary, pronunciation and grammar exercises. Learn the whole, or parts, of the conversation for homework.

11. Next lesson listen again to the tape and repeat the exercises. Do further exercises if it feels necessary, or begin again with a different group of students from the class and make a new conversation following the same procedure above.

Comments Language learning is often controlled by textbooks which can blunt the students' initiative and interest. With this method students can make up their own conversations in the foreign language from the earliest stages of learning. At more advanced levels the conversation can be conducted partly or entirely in L2, with the teacher available as a resource when needed. With practice the recorded material should become more and more meaningful as a basis for language study.

77. Visualisations

Time : a few minutes — 1 lesson   **Level :** all, except beginners

Language skills Free association, free use of any known, or newly-learned, language.

What is a visualisation exercise? An opportunity to relax, and make free language association. It is essential for the teacher to be aware of the fact that the emphasis is on relaxation and reduction of tension, and *no* attempt to "force" language, or indeed to offer any contribution, should be made.

Why are visualisation exercises important? They may be used in language learning for a number of purposes:

- reducing tension and promoting relaxation as a preparation for learning
- promoting learning through fantasy supported by any of the senses: listening, seeing, feeling, and even smelling.

A great deal of language teaching concentrates on the *language* to be taught, but it is equally important to be aware of *learning,* and of the student's personal response to the learning situation. A relaxed student is more likely to learn than one who is tense. Visualisation can help in this process.

Some general points concerning visualisations:

Posture Students should sit or lie in a relaxed posture:

Sitting: both feet flat on the floor, hands lightly resting on the thighs or lightly clasped on the lap, straight back but relaxed neck and shoulders, "light" head ("like a gas-filled balloon" or "as if a thread is pulling it gently towards the ceiling").

Lying: both feet flat on the floor, bent knees, hands resting slightly on stomach, elbows on the floor, head resting on a book or similar hard support about 8 centimetres high.

Students' attitude Don't worry if students feel sleepy or giggle during the exercises — it is a sign that they are releasing built-up tension. If students want to avoid being sleepy, advise them to arch their backs for a while.

Instructions Give clear instructions at the beginning:

> "Sit/lie comfortably//close your eyes//feel your breathing slowing down//"etc.

Avoid instructions like "Imagine. . ." or "Try to imagine. . .". Say "You are walking on the beach", not "Imagine that you are walking on the beach". Construct the exercises so that they include as many of the senses as possible. "The apple" below is a good example of this.

Don't rush, and come back gently:

> "When you are ready//come back//open your eyes//look at your feet//look round the room//stretch//and take a long deep breath."

Remember, the exercise is intended to relax students so you must use only known language. Some students find quiet background music helpful as an aid to relaxation.

Comments Always introduce visualisation exercises to a group who have not done them before by trying a simple, short and undemanding exercise. If you try something too ambitious first, you may create resistance to this kind of exercise. It is more important to choose the vocabulary and grammatical content so it is suitable for the group, and *not* over-demanding. Here are some examples:

Example 1   The apple — 1

"Close your eyes and see an apple. . . (after 1 minute) Open your eyes."

Ask the students to describe their apples in L1 first, if necessary. Was it coloured? What colour(s)? Was it a specific apple? What was it resting on?

Example 2   The apple — 2

"Close your eyes//you are in a familiar setting in which you would enjoy eating an apple//you have a cool, delicious apple in your hand//feel the apple's coolness//its weight//its firmness//its round volume//its smoothness//examine details//see bruises//the way the light sparkles on it//see the many colours on the surface//watch until your mouth waters//bite the apple//hear its juicy snap//feel the juice on your fingers//with a knife, slice the apple to see what's inside//explore it in detail//eat it up. . .".

Example 3   Relax your eyes

This can be used as a break activity, in particular when students have been doing reading or writing activities.

"Close your eyes//see a bird flying from tree to tree//then sitting quietly on a branch//a ball rolling along the ground//then coming to a stop//a rocket being launched//then disappearing into the blue sky//a slow ping-pong match//follow the ball//the match gets faster and faster//until you can't see the ball anymore//a rabbit hopping along. . .".

Example 4   Guided Fantasy

This can be used to consolidate newly acquired language. Write a story or description of a scene which includes the desired language. Choose suitable music to accompany it if this will support the fantasy. Read the story/description for the students.

Example 5   Memories

Remember from your childhood:
> — a much-loved teacher
> — eating an ice-cream cornet
> — your bedroom
> — climbing a tree
> — what you ate for breakfast
> — an old man/woman
> — a family trip
> — going to the seaside/the country
> — a birthday party

Follow up by asking students to describe what they saw, in as much detail as possible — for the whole class or in small groups.

Example 6   Group Fantasy

Group size: large enough to provide diversity and small enough to allow each member to participate actively — five is about right.
In a quiet, undisturbed and preferably dark environment, get students to close eyes and relax, ideally lying like spokes of a wheel with heads toward the centre. Spend several minutes relaxing.
When relaxed, a self-elected member of the group describes a fantasy he or she is having, telling it as an on-going event or state, in full detail. The other members of the group can actively participate in this fantasy episode, for example, by providing sound effects, such as wind, rain, thunder, birds, dogs, etc.
Then another member takes over the role of guide, carrying the fantasy further. Each participant takes over in turn.
The only rule in the game is that no criticism is permitted. Rules of reality may (and should!) be broken.

Comments Visualisation exercises adopt a more whole-person approach to the student in the language classroom. Many traditional language teaching techniques — expecting students to produce language very early in their course, emphasising mistakes and correction, insisting on "correctness", often at the expense of fluency and confidence — have frequently inhibited students' abilities. It is not suggested here that practices such as those described should replace conventional practice, but that teachers should be aware of the student as a person, and aware that the relaxed student is more likely to do well than a student who is intimidated and tense in the class-room. For certain groups, perhaps particularly smaller groups of older students, who have a history of unsuccessful language learning, the occasional visualisation exercise can make a valuable contribution to their overall learning programme.

78. Help yourselves!

Time : One or more lessons   **Level:** All

Language skills Revision activities, depending on material chosen.

Procedure

1. Assemble a variety of revision exercises and materials. Group them and display on a large table or separate tables. The groups may, for example, be as follows:

    — **Word and phrase exercises**
    — **Dialogues**
    — **Listening comprehension exercises**
    — **Discussion activities**

2. Explain what materials and exercises are available.

3. The students *choose* the exercise group they want to work with and go through the material provided, individually or in groups.

4. When one group of exercises is completed, the students can help themselves to the next 'course', as if at a buffet meal.

Comments Materials must be well prepared in advance. Students could participate by helping to write or collect some of the material. Especially suitable for revision purposes or for end-of-term work. Provides a high level of student activity.

79. Team teaching

Time : An occasional lesson or a longer series of lessons

Level : Advanced, higher Intermediate

Language skills Parallel training in L2 and another subject. Understanding, translating, summarising, and answering set questions. Note-taking "skimming" for information from reference texts.

Procedure

1. Two teachers work together — one language teacher and one subject teacher in, for example, geography, history or sports. Planning is done by the two teachers together.

2. The teaching is carried out in both L1 and L2, with the subject teacher supplying the main factual input and the language teacher operating chiefly as translator. Some L2 reference material may be used, perhaps particularly in science subjects.

3. The text material is written in L1 and the students use it to:
   — make summaries in L2
   — answer set questions in L2
   — translate short, important sections into L2 with the help of dictionaries

4. Discuss and evaluate the teaching in the whole class.

Comments Conventional language teaching is based on L2 texts 'for their own sake'. In real life we always use language for a purpose, as a means to an end. Subject integration means there is a *reason* to use the L2. If the motivation for the second subject is high, experience has shown that even the foreign language is acquired more effectively through studying a subject or topic and *using* L2 as a means of communication, rather than studying conventional language texts. A good example of an activity which assists language acquisition.

80. The Block of Flats

Time : Several lessons, including homework tasks. Alternatively, an on-going activity lasting for a whole term.

Level : Intermediate, Advanced

Language skills All skills may be practised through a variety of activities such as: Areas of vocabulary (furniture, jobs, families, etc.); descriptions (people, objects, places, events, etc.); dialogues; role-plays; written exercises (letters, descriptions, note taking, etc.);fact-finding about the country/locality chosen to place the block of flats (local geography, maps, brochures, industry, entertainments, etc.); making reports/presenting information to other students; conventional language exercises based on situations, functions, grammar, vocabulary and phrases.

Procedure

The idea behind this activity is for the class together to build their own miniature community around a block of flats and the people who live in it. There are endless possibilities for development once the framework (building, flats and inhabitants) has been created.

Examples of tasks/activities:

1. **The building:** How many storeys? How many flats? Size of each flat? Small shop — type? etc.

2. **The inhabitants:** How many to each flat? Men/women/children? Animals — pets? etc.

3. **Names? Ages? Occupations? Interests? etc.**

4. **Relations within each flat:** Different family types? Biographies? etc.

5. **Relations between neighbours:** Dialogues on the stairs? Greetings? Complaints? Arguments? Borrowing things? Asking for help? Block party? Tenants' association meeting? etc.

6. **Contact with the outside world:** Telephone conversations? The morning post? The town? Shopping? Entertainments? Sports? Travel? Work? etc.

7. **Incidents:** An accident? A scandal? A crime? A celebration? 10 years later — what has happened? etc.

Comments This activity provides enormous scope for students to use their imagination and creative abilities, both collectively and individually. Work on the project can be done partly in the whole class, partly in small groups and certain tasks either individually or in pairs. Each flat may be represented by one or more students, who gradually assume their new identity. The same basic idea can be used to build up a project around, for example, a workplace, a hotel, a hospital or a pub.

81. Projects

Time : from 1 hour, to several weeks **Level :** Intermediate, Advanced

Language skills Very varied, depending on the exact nature of the project. Most projects involve planning and discussing in small groups (in L2 at more advanced levels), making oral summaries, using reference books, reading and listening comprehension. Many projects end with a written and/or oral presentation of the material studied.

What is a project? A project is any activity in which students spend the majority of time collecting information from a variety of sources, collating the information, and (usually) finally presenting it either to the whole class, or in visual form for other people.
Most projects have an end product — an oral report, poster, file or other written presentation of the information, but the main emphasis of the activity is on finding, collating, and evaluating the information.

A project may take different forms:

a.   **Research** — the students, individually or in small groups, have to find information from, for example, reference books in the school library.

b.   **Questionnaires** — here the students first prepare the questionnaire, and then give it to a number of people, finally collecting and collating the results. A questionnaire project may be done either by interviewing people outside school, within the school, or even, on a smaller scale to introduce the idea of project work, within the class itself.

c.   **Observation** Projects are particularly appropriate if students are visiting the country where the L2 is spoken, or have access to film or video in L2. They have a list of questions to answer which involves them in observing — either facts, information, or specific language items *(What did the man say when he apologised?).*

In most cases, a project results in a group product — a report or poster, the successful completion of which involves each student contributing the results of his or her personal project.

Some general points concerning project work:

Purpose It is essential that each individual or group knows what the project is about, and what their particular contribution is to be.

Materials The teacher needs to check in advance *what* material is needed and *where* it can be found.

122

Activities

Time The teacher should suggest, and discuss with the group, a time plan based on both the shorter and longer term objectives.

Presentation Before the project is started each group should agree *how* the project is to be presented and *by whom*. It may be presented orally, in the form of posters, in a written report, etc. Larger projects usually involve more than one such element, and each individual student or group contributes part of the total presentation.

Group work Most projects are best done if the work is shared by different members of the group. If necessary the group needs to be divided into smaller units. It is an essential part of this work that students and groups recognise that each is trying to help the others. Co-operation is an important feature of the work.

Involvement A project should involve *all* the students, though perhaps in very different ways. Some students can be asked to take notes, illustrate, count the results of questionnaires, present a report etc.
 The teacher, as co-ordinator and motivator, needs to remember that it is the *process* of gathering the information, collating and preparing it which is more important than the presentation. Although the best projects often result in an attractive *product*, it is the preparatory activity which is important.

Comments Information obtained and presented in project form is generally more memorable and involving for the students than more conventional classroom teaching. The opportunity to work in groups, with responsibility for your own work, can also be a rewarding experience for many students.

If students are not used to project work it is advisable to begin with something which is engaging, but will not take too long. Students can easily lose interest if they do not see a result reasonably quickly.

Project work can often provide an excellent opportunity for students to discover more about various aspects of the culture of the country of L2. It can be appropriate, for example, to decide in the whole class on a subject area for a project of this type. It may be connected to the course book, or independent of other studies. Some examples are:

A town or city (buildings, population, history, etc.)
A historical period (dates, main events, famous people of the time, etc.)
Music (details of a singer or band, examples of songs, music and text)
Geographical region (places, towns, industries, traditions, dialect, etc.)
An author (biographical background, dates and details of works, etc)

Procedure

1. Decide with the whole class on the *subject* for the project.

2. Make detailed preparation of what is to be studied , where the information is to be found, questionnaires which may be needed, etc. Make a fairly detailed timetable if the project is to extend more than one or two lessons.

3. Divide the class into appropriate groups to perform the different tasks which will be needed for the full project. Make sure each group is fully aware of the details of its part in the whole plan.

4. Each group collects the material or information it needs. During this time there should be the possibility to consult the teacher, and, for longer projects, for interim discussions in the whole class of progress, problems, the need to change the timetable etc.

5. Each group arranges its material for presentation to the whole class.

6. Each group presents its material to the whole class.

7. If appropriate, the material from different groups is collated and arranged for final presentation.

8. The full project is presented — perhaps to the rest of the school, or parents, in a poster exhibition etc.

9. After the project is finished, students discuss what they did, whether it was successful, what they learnt, difficulties they encountered , and, if appropriate, ideas for a future project.

82. Evaluations

Time : 20-40 minutes **Level :** All

Language skills This activity is recommended to be conducted in L1 so students can easily express what they think of the classwork and their language studies.

Procedure.

1. The teacher gives the students a list of language activities that have been practised during the course. The students are asked to mark against each one either "enjoyed", "all right" or "didn't like".

Examples (the teacher can choose from a list, add other activities, and if necessary translate the questionaire into L1)

	enjoyed	all right	didn't like
Reading texts	☐	☐	☐
Writing exercises	☐	☐	☐
Listening to tapes/teacher	☐	☐	☐
Talking/discussing/asking questions	☐	☐	☐
Practising vocabulary	☐	☐	☐
Practising phrases	☐	☐	☐
Practising grammar	☐	☐	☐
Working with the course book	☐	☐	☐
Working with authentic material	☐	☐	☐
Doing project work	☐	☐	☐
Doing role-plays	☐	☐	☐
Doing language games	☐	☐	☐
Working individually	☐	☐	☐
Working in pairs/groups	☐	☐	☐
Working in the whole class led by the teacher	☐	☐	☐

2. The teacher then writes some questions on the board to help the students to evaluate some aspects of their language studies. Each student writes anonymously on a separate piece of paper. The responses to the list of activities above could provide some help in answering these questions.

Example questions:

— **What has been most successful?**
— **What has not worked well?**
— **What would you like more of?**
— **What would you prefer to have less of?**
— **What would you like to repeat because you didn't understand?**
— **What suggestions can you make for improvements?**

Students should be encouraged to write spontaneously and to take up both positive and negative points.

3. The pieces of paper are collected in and shuffled.

4. The teacher writes three headings on the board:
      Good   *Bad*   *Suggestions*

5. The teacher then reads out each piece of paper in turn and summarises under the three columns on the board.

6. Discuss the results in the whole class, draw conclusions, and make plans for the future work.

Comments Encourages students to take some responsibility for their own programme of study and to realise that evaluation is an important part of language learning. The two introductory parts of the activity (points 1 and 2) could be done separately (only the activity list or only the questions) or combined to give a fuller evaluation.

What can be changed? This will of course depend on a number of factors such as timetable and syllabus, the availability of materials, the type of course book used, and so on. On the other hand an evaluation of this kind can certainly influence studies positively and give the students an important feeling of participation in the planning of their language studies. It is, of course, important to see that comments and suggestions are followed up.

Variation As well as the course of study, students can be asked their opinion of their own language skills using question like:

How good do you think you are at these different things in (L2):

	Good	Satisfactory	Poor
Pronunciation			
Reading			
Vocabulary/phrases			
Writing/summarising			
Conversation			
Giving a talk			

The list of skills can be translated, and items can be added or removed depending on the programme the students have followed.

Answer to examples in Activity 12: If I see her, I'll ask her. We won't need our umbrellas.

DATE